Kentucky
WEATHER

Kentucky WEATHER

JERRY HILL

with a foreword by

T. G. SHUCK

THE UNIVERSITY PRESS OF KENTUCKY

Publication of this volume was made possible in part
by a grant from the National Endowment for the Humanities.

Scholarly publisher for the Commonwealth,
serving Bellarmine University, Berea College, Centre
College of Kentucky, Eastern Kentucky University,
The Filson Historical Society, Georgetown College,
Kentucky Historical Society, Kentucky State University,
Morehead State University, Murray State University,
Northern Kentucky University, Transylvania University,
University of Kentucky, University of Louisville,
and Western Kentucky University.

Editorial and Sales Offices:
The University Press of Kentucky
663 South Limestone Street, Lexington, Kentucky 40508-4008
www.kentuckypress.com

09 08 07 06 05   5 4 3 2 1

Acknowledgment is made to Dick Gilbreath for his assistance in
generating many of the maps and figures that appear in this book.

Library of Congress Cataloging-in-Publication Data
Hill, Jerry D., 1937–
Kentucky weather / Jerry Hill ;
with a foreword by T.G. Shuck.
p.   cm.
Includes bibliographical references and index.
ISBN 0-8131-2351-8 (hardcover : alk. paper)
1. —Kentucky Climate. I. Title.
QC984.K4H55 2005
551.69769—dc22   2004026888

This book is printed on acid-free recycled paper meeting
the requirements of the American National Standard
for Permanence in Paper for Printed Library Materials.

∞ ✪

Manufactured in the United States of America.

Member of the Association of American University Presses

To Jean,

who has been a faithful

weatherman's wife for so many years.

And to Jeri and Jeff,

who were there when this

entire project was started.

Thanks for your support over

all the years.

Our mentioning of the weather ... [is] perhaps not idle.

Perhaps we have a deep and legitimate need to know in our entire being

what the day is like, to see it and feel it, to know how the sky is grey,

paler in the south, with patches of blue in the southwest, with snow on

the ground, the thermometer at 18, and cold wind making your ears

ache. I have a real need to know these things because I myself am part

of the weather and part of the climate and part of the place, and a day

in which I have not shared truly in all this is no day at all.

FATHER THOMAS MERTON,

GETHSEMANI ABBEY,

TRAPPIST, KENTUCKY

Contents

Figures

Tables

Foreword

T. G. SHUCK

Chief Meteorologist, WKYT-TV, Lexington, Kentucky

As I think back, the images are still vivid. Snapshots frozen in time, forever burned in my memory: the darkest, most threatening sky I've ever seen; the door of our church blown wide open by howling winds; driving home through a pitch-dark neighborhood; the crackle of the radio as the announcer spoke of tornadoes throughout the area and many deaths in the commonwealth; my entire family sleeping downstairs on a pull-out bed not knowing whether a tornado would strike in the middle of the night.

It was April 3, 1974, the day Mother Nature unleashed her wrath with deadly force. As a scared little boy just days shy of my sixth birthday, I hoped that night only to see the light of day the next morning. You can imagine my relief when I finally woke up from a restless sleep to see the beautiful sunshine streaming through our living-room window.

The Super Outbreak, as it came to be known, was truly amazing. Thirteen states saw 148 tornadoes in 48 hours. Hundreds of people were killed, thousands were injured, and many communities were reduced to rubble. The landscape was literally changed forever. So was weather technology: the outbreak spurred lifesaving innovations. The storm also changed people, who grew more aware of the weather and the unforeseen effect it could have on their lives.

My family was fortunate. None of us were injured, and we suffered no property damage. Still, the storm had a dramatic impact on my life. It gave me my first lesson in mortality—and at an early age. It was *the* weather event that sparked my interest in meteorology. From that day on I became fascinated with all things related to the weather and how it worked. Somehow I knew that it would become a lifelong obsession. And it eventually led me to a career in television weather here in my native Kentucky.

The historic storm also made me marvel, even at that young age, how the weather could be so violent one day and so beautiful and calm the next. Anyone who has paid any attention to the weather in Kentucky has learned to expect quick changes. The old saying, "If you don't like the weather, just wait a minute," definitely rings true.

These are among the many words of wisdom, from factual to folkloric, that you will find in the pages of this book. If you observe Kentucky's weather long enough, you become keenly aware of intricate regional variations in climate and their effect on the weather. From the Pennyrile region in western Kentucky to the coalfields of eastern Kentucky, the weather and the climate are the same in no two places even when they appear to be the same everywhere.

Jerry Hill does a masterly job of explaining not only how the weather works here in Kentucky and across the United States but also why conditions vary from region to region across our great commonwealth. Other books on weather history and climate are, unfortunately, long on numbers and short on explanations. *Kentucky Weather* is a perfect mix of both. It provides a wealth of data as well as accessible but thorough explanations of Kentucky weather past and present. In *Kentucky Weather* you will find chapters dealing with temperature, rain, snow and ice, floods, severe storms, and drought. You will also learn about the effect of the weather on the history and development of Kentucky, concepts of and stories about Kentucky weather dating back to the first explorers and settlers, and associated folklore and superstition. Most of the historic climate data archived in Kentucky's reporting stations dates back only to the late 1800s. Kentucky Weather goes back even further, drawing on the books and diaries of colonial-era weather observers.

There is a reason that so many people are interested in the weather. It affects everyone twenty-four hours a day, seven days a week, and all year round. It is inescapable. And its unpredictability is fascinating. Everyone from the self-proclaimed "weather nerd" to the casual observer of daily conditions will come away from this book with a better understanding of Kentucky's weather. There is nothing like it anywhere.

Preface

Weather is probably the single most important factor controlling our daily activities, and, while we try to understand it as best we can, it continually frustrates us with its restlessness, then awes us with its beauty. Weather can cause happiness or melancholy, poverty or prosperity, tragedy or good fortune, idleness or industry, but it never brings boredom to Kentuckians. Weather and its vagaries are a way of life, an intimate part of the Kentucky lifestyle, not because the weather is unpredictable, but because it's dynamic.

Weather is like a restless child—to know it is to love it. But too often we try to know it only as lines on today's weather map or as a report of yesterday's temperature extremes. Set deeper within the weather are countless ways in which it shaped the history, the geology, and the personality of the Bluegrass State. Over the ages, the weather was responsible for the conditions that produced Kentucky's wealth of coal deposits and made the region a spa for residents of the Deep South seeking refuge from the oppressive summer heat. And, in at least one case, it was a decisive factor in defeating an Indian attack. Within the report of a single extreme weather event are countless personal experiences.

Readers who desire detailed statistics about Kentucky's climate may find that this book partially satisfies their appetite, but they will, I hope, also find that it is an interesting review of the weather as it has influenced Kentucky's development and shaped its lifestyle. Perhaps it will answer some of their questions about whether the weather has influenced a certain aspect of Kentucky life, but, for every question it answers, it will most likely raise another. At best, it will spur others to investigate in detail how to plan in order to coexist in harmony with Kentucky weather.

Acknowledgments

The material presented in this book is the result of the efforts of hundreds of people who have worked so diligently over the years to observe and document Kentucky weather. These include not only the professionals working in the field but also, and especially, all the unpaid volunteer observers who contribute their daily weather readings. The work of all these people is deeply appreciated.

I also wish especially to acknowledge the help of several who assisted in providing data for this book. At the Kentucky Climate Center, located at Western Kentucky University, Dr. Stuart Foster, who serves as the state climatologist, provided assistance. I owe special thanks to Glen Conner, the state climatologist emeritus, for some of his descriptions of notable weather events. Tom Priddy, the director of the Kentucky Agricultural Weather Center at the University of Kentucky, provided assistance and continues to provide outstanding weather services to Kentuckians. The staff members of the libraries at the University of Kentucky, the Filson Historical Society, the University of Louisville, and Western Kentucky University were helpful in identifying some of the material related to early Kentucky weather.

Meteorologist Norm Reitmeyer and his colleagues at the National Weather Service (NWS) office in Louisville reviewed the manuscript and provided useful comments. Thanks also to staff members at the NWS offices in Paducah and Jackson for their help in providing material.

Much of the data in the tables was provided by the Midwestern Regional Climate Center and the National Oceanic and Atmospheric Administration's National Climatic Data Center. Some of the material used herein and credited to agencies of the U.S. government is publicly available and, as provided under 17 U.S.C. §403, not subject to copyright protection.

Finally, special credit should go to my copyeditor, Joseph Brown, who struggled mightily to improve the writing of this old weatherman, whose prose for many years went only slightly beyond "partly cloudy and warm."

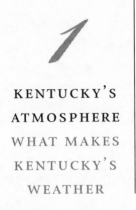

KENTUCKY'S ATMOSPHERE
WHAT MAKES KENTUCKY'S WEATHER

Over the millions of square miles of land surface on the face of the earth can be found a seemingly infinite variety of climates. In the extreme southern portion of the United States, there is a relatively stable climate, one broken in its monotony only by the occasional tropical storm. In the Pacific Northwest, there are frequent low-pressure systems moving onshore to bring wind, rain, and persistent cloud cover. Some of the higher elevations, especially in the western United States, receive abundant precipitation and often remain snow covered year-round, not because of migrating weather systems, but because of the elevation.

In Kentucky, the weather is influenced by both passing storms and elevation differences. The location of the state—in a latitude where low-pressure centers (cyclones) and high-pressure centers (anticyclones) are common—has the major influence on the weather patterns. A belt of winds aloft moving from west to east around the globe steers the low-pressure centers, which bring stormy weather. The wind circulation works in conjunction with the underlying terrain to induce the intensification or dissipation of storms. Between the major low-pressure centers are the high-pressure centers, which bring periods of fair weather.

During the winter months, the belt of westerly winds intensifies, causing the paths of the low-pressure centers to move as far south as the southern United States. These lows often pass through

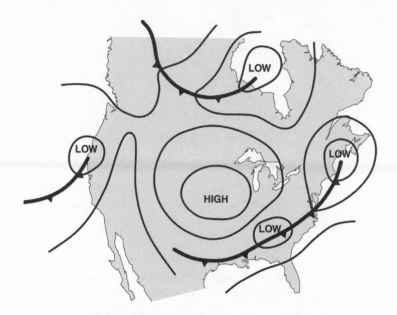

FIGURE 1. *A typical winter weather map, showing a low-pressure center moving across the southeastern United States toward the Atlantic Coast with a cold high-pressure center from Canada following into the Ohio Valley behind it.*
(Data provided by Kentucky Agricultural Experiment Station.)

or near Kentucky, bringing frequent and abrupt changes in the weather. The old saying, "If you don't like the weather, just wait a minute," has often been voiced by Kentuckians, who learn to expect such rapid changes. Not surprisingly, the saying is common across the central United States, where similarly drastic weather fluctuations occur.

After the passage of a winter low-pressure center, the winds often shift to the north, bringing a large mass of cold air from Canada. Such cold air masses can usually be located on the weather map as large high-pressure centers. As they move from the cold, snow-covered interior of Canada or Alaska, they are gradually modified by the warmer ground, but they can still produce bone-chilling, subzero weather by the time they reach Kentucky.

As the warmer seasons of the year develop, the low-pressure centers become less frequent in Kentucky, their favored path across the United States being more commonly drawn north near the Canadian border. In the summer, the semipermanent high pressure that usually persists across the South Atlantic extends its influence into the southeastern United States. It effectively blocks out most of the moving low-pressure systems but is responsible for establishing a wind pattern that brings ample moisture from the Gulf of Mexico into the Mississippi and Ohio Valleys. The moisture from the Gulf region aids in the development of summer showers and thunderstorms, the source of most summer rainfall in Kentucky. Occasionally, the Atlantic high pressure intensifies across the entire southern United States, effectively blocking even the Gulf moisture out of Kentucky. This pattern most commonly develops in late summer or early fall, resulting in a minimum of cloud cover and what is normally the driest time of the year.

The passage of a high- or low-pressure center is marked, not only by the characteristic weather, but also by barometric fluctuations. But barometric fluctuations do not always mean what amateur weather enthusiasts think they mean. The pressure ranges of barometers made for home use are often equipped with indications of the type of weather to be expected (*fair, stormy, rainy,* etc.), indications that can be misleading because they do not represent absolute forecasts. The real value of barometers is found when they are used to track changes in pressure over a 6–12-hour period. Substantially falling pressure normally implies that low pressure and, probably, precipitation are approaching; strongly rising pressure, that the center of the low has passed and clearing should follow. During the summer months, when few low- or high-pressure systems migrate through the Ohio Valley, a barometer needle can remain nearly motionless for weeks at a time. The highest pressure ever recorded at an official weather station in Kentucky was 30.99 inches of mercury (1,049.4 millibars) at Louisville on February 12, 1981. The lowest was 28.94 inches of mercury (980.0 millibars), also at Louisville, on February 28, 1902. (These are pressures that have been corrected to sea level by adjusting for

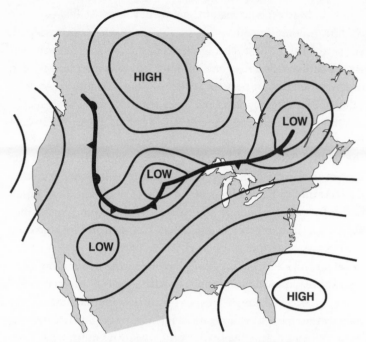

FIGURE 2. *A typical summer weather map showing how fronts remain mostly to the north and moisture is directed from the Gulf of Mexico into the Ohio Valley. (Data provided by Kentucky Agricultural Experiment Station.)*

elevation. This is necessary so that all reports from across the country can be compared on the same basis to find the locations of high- and low-pressure systems.)

On rare occasions, Kentucky will be affected by the remnants of a tropical storm that is moving north from the Gulf Coast. Tropical storms and hurricanes are large storms that develop far out to sea, usually between June and November. Their winds—which can cause substantial damage when they make landfall—usually dissipate a short distance inland. Still, the remnants of these storms often persist as low-pressure centers, bringing cloud cover and rain as they move through interior portions of the country.

When forecasters are looking for adverse weather, the routinely passing low-pressure centers generate the most interest because they create the rising motions of the air that, in turn, produce widespread clouds and precipitation. The availability of moisture to a low-pressure system is a major factor in determining the amount of precipitation it will bring. Although many of the lows reaching Kentucky originate over the Pacific Ocean, little Pacific moisture is carried beyond the Great Plains. The source of about 80% of the moisture falling in Kentucky is the Gulf of Mexico, with only about 20% from the Pacific Ocean. A very small additional amount—noticeable only as snow flurries traveling on cold northerly winter winds—comes from the Great Lakes. Even though Kentucky has numerous lakes and rivers, the moisture that they add to the air is not significant.

Kentucky is an ideal place for those who enjoy seeing the ever-changing designs that clouds paint in the sky. The moisture associated with the weather systems creates a variety of cloud types and patterns that often give hints to coming weather. When there are no active systems, skies will sometimes be dotted with small, fluffy cumulus clouds that develop during the day and dissipate by evening. These are typically considered fair-weather clouds, and they form when the air rises as a result of daytime heating.

Typically, cold fronts entering the state from the north or the northwest are preceded by clouds that slowly become thicker and denser as the front approaches. As the air near the front is forced up, showers can develop and even thunderstorms form in a band along or ahead of the front. A band of thunderstorms with severe weather that has formed slightly ahead of a front is called a *squall line*. The skies usually clear a few hours after the front passes, and cooler, drier air follows in its wake.

Warm fronts often develop in the cooler months, whenever winds shift to the south and bring warmer air north. As the warm, humid air moves over colder ground, the moisture condenses and causes widespread cloud cover. Drizzle, fog, and light rain can persist for several days when warm fronts approach the state. If a warm front moves over ground the temperature of which is below

FIGURE 3. *Cumulus clouds are typical of fair weather.*

freezing, dangerous icestorms can occur. In an icestorm, the rain or drizzle that falls freezes on contact with cold surfaces, resulting in hazardous driving conditions, and can also cause large trees or power lines to fall.

Air can be lifted, not only by the rising motion of fronts, but also by being forced against a large terrain barrier. Most mountain barriers have more precipitation on the upwind side, but Kentucky does not have anything that might be considered a large, extensive barrier. The knobs that surround the Bluegrass region are irregular and rise only 300–500 feet above the terrain. Since they do not form a solid barrier, air moves around them easily, and it is unlikely that they significantly modify the precipitation pattern in the state.

The mountainous eastern portion of the state is actually an old eroded plateau. The terrain is irregular, but its elevation variations—at most 500 feet between valley and ridge top—do not significantly enhance rainfall amounts. The only mountain ridges that are substantial are Pine Mountain and Black Mountain, extending northeast–southwest near the Virginia border. For the 2-year period 1940–42, rainfall observations were taken at a site at the 4,000-foot elevation atop Black Mountain near Lynch. Monthly

FIGURE 4. *Altostratus clouds are usually forerunners of precipitation.*
(National Oceanic and Atmospheric Administration/
Department of Commerce.)

rainfall totals were generally very similar to amounts recorded at
nearby valley sites. Under certain wind conditions, there would
necessarily be increased rainfall on the ridge, and such circumstances apparently prevailed during July 1941, when the mountain
station reported over 17 inches of rainfall but stations in the rest of
southeastern Kentucky averaged only 6–10 inches.

The topography of the state does not seem to have a significant
influence on the temperature patterns that are observed. Normally,
the average temperature can be expected to be reduced by about
4°F per 1,000 feet of additional elevation if all other factors remain
unchanged. Even though elevation ranges from about 300 feet
above sea level in the extreme southwest to around 1,500 feet in the
eastern counties, large temperature differences are not apparent
in the records. This is primarily because few observing stations
are at higher elevations. Most are between 500 and 1,000 feet,
having been established in such easily accessible locations as
along roads and in towns in valleys. The result is that variations in
altitude among observing locations across the state usually account for a difference of only about 2°F in annual average temperatures. However, at high ridge-top locations in eastern Kentucky,

FIGURE 5. *Cumulonimbus are thunderstorm clouds
and can cause severe weather.
(National Oceanic and Atmospheric Administration/
Department of Commerce.)*

temperatures can be expected to be colder than those officially recorded for the area.

The general temperature pattern across Kentucky shows that
the long-term annual averages decline from about 58°F in the
southwest portion of the state to about 54°F in the northeast. This
variation seems to be influenced by a combination of latitude and
elevation. The influence of elevation on temperature is evident at
isolated locations, such as the top of Black Mountain in Harlan
County, where snow is more predominant during the winter than
anywhere else in the state. Colder temperatures on the mountain
often favor precipitation in the form of snow there at the same
time that rain is falling at valley locations. The favorable conditions for snow at Black Mountain were instrumental in the development of a short-lived ski area there in the early 1970s.

The shape of Kentucky, which places its shortest dimension
north–south, makes it somewhat different than its neighbors
across the Ohio River. There is only about a 4°F difference in the

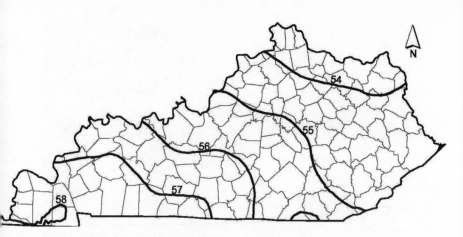

FIGURE 6. *Normal mean annual temperature (°F) in Kentucky*
(based on 1971–2000 data).
(Kentucky Climate Center.)

mean annual temperature across the state. However, in Illinois, the distance from the northern to the southern extremity is 360 miles, and the mean annual temperature ranges from 49°F to 59°F. Kentucky's relative homogeneity in temperatures is an advantage because the state's businesses do not have to cater to a wide range of climatic requirements.

Like that of average temperature, the pattern of average annual precipitation in Kentucky runs from southwest to northeast. Annual totals vary from about 55 inches in the southwest to about 43 inches in the northeast. There are two factors likely responsible for this effect. Probably the most important is the increasing distance from the Gulf of Mexico as one travels north in the state. The most abundant precipitation falls where moisture is most ample, and the supply of moisture decreases with distance from the Gulf. But also important are the cooler temperatures in the northern sections, which reduce the ability of the air to hold moisture, thereby limiting precipitation.

Details about Kentucky weather have been included in tables and figures that constitute the appendix to this book. A selected group of twenty-nine locations for which long-term weather

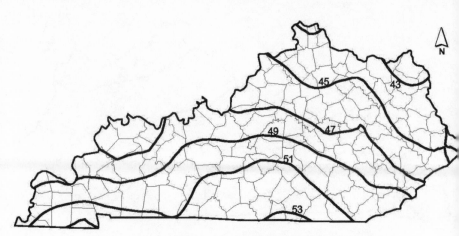

FIGURE 7. *Normal mean annual precipitation (inches) in Kentucky (based on 1971–2000 data). (Kentucky Climate Center.)*

observations are available has been used to give details about averages and extremes observed throughout the state. The locations are shown in figure 8.

While the gross overall pattern of Kentucky's climate can be determined from the historical weather records, there are many local factors that can cause minor variations. The microclimate of a field, a house, or a farm depends on the local topography, vegetation, soil type, and many other interacting factors. Kentucky's irregular terrain is ideal for the production of many different local climates. Hills and valleys are particularly noted for their influence on climate. Environments on north-facing slopes tend to be colder, being shaded from the sun for a portion of the day, especially in the winter months, when the sun is normally at a low angle. Environments on south-facing slopes tend to be warmer, receiving more direct sunlight during the course of the day. And the temperature differences can be great enough that plants on south-facing slopes can bloom as much as 2 weeks earlier than those on north-facing slopes.

Probably the best-known effect of terrain in producing a microclimate is the existence of "frost pockets." Nearly everyone has seen

FIGURE 8. *Locations of Kentucky weather stations for which data are given in the appendix.*

frost in isolated depressions early on mornings that are cool but not quite cold enough for a widespread frost. These frost pockets form because, as air cools, it becomes heavier and gravity causes it to settle to the lowest-lying parts of the terrain, where minimum temperature readings can be 5°F–10°F colder than they are on a hilltop. Frost pockets are more common in Kentucky than in many other states because of Kentucky's higher proportion of irregular terrain.

Local climatic variations can also be caused by urban development, which serves to concentrate sources of heat. Concrete, brick, and asphalt absorb heat during the day and release it slowly at night, tending to keep minimum temperatures higher in the city. This has become known to meteorologists as the *urban heat island effect.* In a city the size of Louisville, the average annual difference in mean temperature between the downtown area and the surrounding rural countryside can be as much as 2°F–3°F. Of course, the difference is greatest during the winter heating season. In smaller cities, the difference is more likely to be less than 1°F. Weather observations are preferably taken in suburban or rural areas to avoid just such artificially elevated temperatures.

In considering all the factors that influence Kentucky's climate, it is natural to wonder whether there is another like it anywhere in the world. Climatologists have devised numerous methods to compare world climates, and one of the most widely used was developed by the German climatologist and amateur botanist Wladimir Köppen early in the twentieth century. Köppen's system classifies the climate of a location on the basis of average annual precipitation, average monthly precipitation, and average monthly temperature, and, according to it, Kentucky's is a mild midlatitude climate with no dry season and a hot summer. As it turns out, most of the southeastern United States is characterized by just this type of climate. Similar climates are to be found in North Korea, eastern China, the east-central coast of Australia, and the northern part of the main island of Japan.

WEATHER
THROUGH
THE AGES

We study climate because we assume that average weather conditions provide a good starting point from which to make long-range weather forecasts. Lacking a specific weather forecast for, say, next Christmas or next summer, we can still make a pretty good estimate of future weather just by studying the records from the past. Of course, there are fluctuations in those records, but variations around the average condition help us identify the extreme conditions that we might need to plan for.

This approach is generally sound if we are making plans for the lifetime of a house, a reservoir, or anything that must stand up under long-term weather extremes. If, however, we look at climate over a longer period of time than just the hundred or so years for which records exist, we soon discover that it is not permanent, that it changes as dramatically as the developments that shape the earth. The evidence of the extremes of climate is visible throughout Kentucky and ranges from coalfields, formed during tropical climates, to the Ohio River, shaped by glaciers along the northern border of the state.

The recent history of Kentucky's weather is written in the official forms used by weather observers during the past hundred years. Earlier notes about the weather are written in the diaries of early settlers and the journals of the first explorers, but, even before the first human cultures arrived in Kentucky, a record of the weather conditions was being written by the rocks, by the soil, and by the streams. Although not as specific as entries made on paper, these geologic clues to past climate can still provide a fascinating report.

One of the most visible signs of a past climate in Kentucky different from the present is the state's vast coal reserves. The coalfields of North America were laid down 250–280 million years ago under a warm, humid climate. We know this because, by studying the coal, which is highly condensed plant matter, we can determine the conditions under which the plants that formed it grew. The absence of rings in the fossilized wood found in Kentucky coal indicates little seasonal variation in temperature and, therefore, tropical or subtropical conditions.

The shapes and the locations of the earth's continents were different when the coal was being formed, and at that time the equator passed near what is now the United States—putting Kentucky in a climate typical of Central Africa. The western edge of the Mississippi Valley bordered a large sea extending to the south. What is now Kentucky was part of a heavily forested coastal plain that sloped gently to the south and southwest, providing a lift to the moist air that came in off the sea. That moist air, combined with the warm temperatures, meant abundant rains, and the forest floor was a spongy mass of half-decayed plant matter that eventually formed the Appalachian coalfields. Over the ages, Kentucky was alternately covered by the sea and lifted again from the water after layers of limestone were built up. Until at least 50 million years ago, tropical forests predominated whenever the region was exposed. The deposition of the coal finally stopped when the sea encroached on the swamp and saltwater killed the vegetation.

Another likely sign of a tropical climate in Kentucky is the formations of coral reef limestone present in ancient seaways. At the falls of the Ohio in Louisville, the river has cut through a section of one of these coral reefs, providing a display of fossilized prehistoric sea life. Since present-day coral cannot survive at water temperatures very far below 65°F, the presence of such deposits would seem to indicate substantially warmer conditions when the fossilized coral was alive. Biologists caution, however, that the species of coral exposed by the Ohio are extinct and could have been adapted to cooler conditions than coral living today. Still, while the presence of fossilized coral cannot pinpoint a specific temperature, it is a strong indication of the mildness of the climate at one point in the past.

The climate of North America up to 100 million years ago is suspected to have been milder and more uniform than it has been since. There is some evidence of widespread glaciation about 700 million years ago. But, in general, continental glaciers were rare until about 100 million years ago, when the average midlatitude land temperature—about 70°F at that point—began a steady decline. When it reached 45°F 2 or 3 million years ago, the great ice age began. In the Northern Hemisphere, glaciers covered a third of the present land area and were found far south of where they can be found today. In the central United States, an ice sheet 1,000–2,000 feet thick covered the Great Lakes and the upper Midwest. There were four major glacial advances and recessions as the temperature alternately warmed and cooled slightly. The second of these, called the *Illinois glacial stage,* which ended about 130,000 years ago, pushed the farthest south and actually reached into Kentucky. There are signs of glacial material extending from near Louisville through the Covington area to around Augusta.

During these cold glacial periods, the climate of Kentucky was certainly cooler than it is today, but the rivers and streams continued to flow free of ice for a portion of the year. Prior to the Illinois glacial stage, the Ohio River extended from its junction with the Mississippi back to around Carrollton. The Kentucky, Licking, and Big Sandy Rivers flowed north into what is now Ohio and Indiana. The ice sheet advanced south and dammed the north-flowing streams, effectively making finger lakes of them. The run-off from rains plus meltwater from the glaciers flooded these lakes, causing their backwaters to grow and, finally, join together across the low places that divided them. The final result was a series of connected lakes that formed the Ohio River valley now along the northern border of Kentucky.

At the time of the glaciers' farthest advance south, there was apparently a sharp dividing line between the climate of the ice sheet and that of the region adjoining it. Certainly, the ice-free region that is now Kentucky was, as we have seen, colder than it is today, but probably not an arctic tundra. It could well have been covered with a boreal, or northern, pine forest. This possibility is supported by the discovery of layers of pine needles in sediment deposits.

During the Illinois glacial stage, the belt of strong westerly winds that is now normally found over southern Canada and the northern United States would have been displaced south across the southern United States. These westerlies are usually the path taken by the frequent midlatitude storms, which would, therefore, have influenced Kentucky's weather much more then than they do today and most likely resulted in precipitation greater than the amount indicated by present observations.

The last glaciation spread into the Ohio Valley about 70,000 years ago and started to retreat about 14,000 years ago. As the ice melted and the glaciers retreated, water returned to the oceans, lakes, and rivers. During the past 200,000 years, sea level has risen and fallen as much as 300 feet, which could help explain some of the incursions of seawater into Kentucky—which, at its lowest, along the Mississippi River in Fulton County, is only 237 feet above sea level—as worldwide glaciation varied.

Even when compared to such dramatic events as extensive volcanic eruption, the uplifting of the land, and the drifting of the continents, the drastic cooling of the earth that resulted in the last great ice age is still considered by many geologists to be one of the most astonishing events in the history of the earth. A number of theories have been proposed to explain it, but none of them can alone account for the kind of cooling necessary to produce such extensive glaciation. The matter is complicated by the fact that the four separate advances of the ice sheet occurred at slightly irregular intervals, indicating that, whatever the causes, those advances were not precisely cyclic.

One possible cause of the cooling trend is variation in the amount of energy, or heat, received from the sun. Most hypotheses developed from this perspective explain temperature variation in terms of either changes in the distance between the earth and the sun, variations in the transparency of the earth's atmosphere to the sun's rays, or differences in the nature of the earth's surface causing sometimes more and sometimes less of the sun's energy to be reflected. Records of solar energy do not, however, go far enough back in time to allow any certain judgment. Another possible cause is continental drift. The theory here is that the continents have simply moved from one climatic region into another. This is plausible since, as we have seen, there is evidence that Kentucky was in an equatorial region at one time.

The glaciers themselves did not dramatically alter the Kentucky landscape. It was, instead, mostly the effects of climate that shaped the land and developed the soil, so change therefore occurred over a very long period. A short distance below the soil surface are very old layers of rock, which have been alternately inundated by the sea, uplifted by a shifting earth, and eroded by the weather. This erosion has worn away some of the rock layers formed during Kentucky's early history, so many of the clues to ancient climate are missing. For instance, there are no traces in the geologic profile of extensive evaporation beds that were laid down elsewhere during periods of very dry desert climates.

In portions of Kentucky, the geologic profile does reveal the influence of the ice age in forming some of the state's best soils. A layer of topsoil known as *loess* covers portions of western Kentucky to a depth of 40 feet in some places, and thin traces of it are evident as far east as the Bluegrass region. The loess is composed of very small silt-sized particles that originally settled out of the meltwater streams along the edge of the ice sheet. At low water levels, when the exposed streambeds became powdery, the loess was picked up by the wind. Very strong, cold winds are known to blow off glaciers, and, during the ice ages, these helped displace the tiny particles, which were carried long distances by the prevailing westerly winds. Some of these deposits were laid down 45,000–50,000 years ago, and, while they are fragile, those soils still form some of Kentucky's finest farmland.

In general, the soils in Kentucky are indicative of a past climate that was reasonably wet. There could, of course, have been periods when rainfall was slight and streams dried up, but, over the past 50,000 years or so, rainfall amounts have probably been as ample as those of today. Certainly, the eroded Cumberland Plateau, which evolved in eastern Kentucky 10–20 million years ago, could not have been formed without ample rainfall.

Rainfall also assisted in the weathering processes that formed the natural bridges seen in eastern Kentucky. Those natural bridges that were formed on ridge tops developed when the soft stone beneath a harder cap was eroded away, leaving an overlying arch. Other bridges were formed when an ample stream flow cut into soft stone above a waterfall and then broke through the face of the falls. In these cases, hard stone that previously formed the edge of the falls left an isolated arch over the stream as erosion gradually moved the waterfall farther upstream.

Clues to past climates can often be drawn from the vegetation known to have grown in a region, as we saw in the example introduced earlier of the fossilized tropical plants found in the coalfields. Over long periods of relatively stable weather conditions, a characteristic ground cover will develop and change very little. This is called the *climax vegetation* and consists of either large trees, prairie grass, or desert scrub, depending on soil conditions, temperature, and available moisture.

The explorers who reached Kentucky from the eastern states in the late eighteenth century reported finding in some places the very large trees normally characteristic of climates with ample rainfall, generally exceeding 30–40 inches per year. What was remarkable about those trees was that, over the years, they had attained such size even on the gravelly soils of the old Cumberland Plateau. Those soils, which developed from sandstone and shale, have a limited water-holding capacity and, thus, no appreciable drought tolerance. The only way in which such forests could have thrived would have been with ample and dependable rainfall.

Those early explorers also found open meadows and canebrakes covering extensive portions of the area that we now call the Bluegrass region. A very large prairie stretching from Owensboro to Bowling Green was almost totally devoid of trees, a fact that earned it the name the Barrens. That prairie was even noted as grasslands on maps prepared by French explorers as early as 1719, when Kentucky was part of the Louisiana Territory. Was climate a factor in producing these anomalies in the climax vegetation present before early settlement began? Certainly, it could not have been poor soil that limited the growth of trees since that region is now one of the most agriculturally productive in the state.

Timothy Taylor, a former grassland ecologist and professor at the University of Kentucky, has discussed with me his belief that other pressures on the ecology of the Barrens kept it as grasslands. According to Taylor, large fires could certainly have destroyed the trees, but the very great number of wild animals present could have been the key factor. Bison, elk, and deer were abundant, and deer are characteristic browsers, nipping the tender starts and shoots of young trees. Elk and bison grazing the meadows could also keep them as devoid of trees as the finest pastures we see today.

It is interesting to note that once the wild animal populations declined—as they did very rapidly after 1800—trees began to appear in the grasslands. Rainfall and soil conditions were apparently adequate. Few trees growing in this region today are older than 200 years.

When the first human cultures arrived in Kentucky 8,000–10,000 years ago, they most likely found a climate somewhat warmer than today's. The gradual warming process that ended the last ice age and caused the glaciers to retreat reached its maximum about 6,000 years ago. This period is called the *climatic optimum*, and, during it, temperatures are estimated to have averaged 5°F above those experienced at present. The temperature afterward declined until the onset of what is called the *little ice age*, which lasted from 1550 to 1850. That period of cooler temperatures over the Northern Hemisphere ended the cultivation of grapes in England and resulted in the advance of the Greenland ice cap, wiping out the prosperous Viking colonies that had been established there in the tenth century.

It is not apparent just what effects fluctuations in climate had on the early Indian cultures in Kentucky, but, whatever they were, they were apparently slight. Sometimes drastic changes in migration patterns or lifestyles can be clues to shifting climate, but no such clues are obvious in existing anthropological evidence. All that is known is that, even though the Indians were primarily hunter-gatherers, they did occasionally practice a primitive form of agriculture. The existence of adequate rainfall to sustain cover and feed for wild animals would also allow the dependable growth of a crop of corn.

The clues to the past climate are almost endless, and many are as contradictory as others are definitive. Thanks to the work of geologists and anthropologists, we continue to learn more about our climatically diverse distant past, but we will never have the detail that has been chronicled since the first settlers arrived.

EARLY
CONCEPTS OF
KENTUCKY'S
WEATHER

The notion of paradise has been present in men's minds for millennia. Sometimes, as in the Garden of Eden of the Christian tradition, it is a paradise on earth, a primordial paradise lost. Other times, as in both the Isles of the Blessed and Olympus, the mountain of the gods, of Greek mythology, it is a present but distant reality. But what all these imagined regions have in common is that they are gardens—characterized by luxuriant vegetation, flowing rivers, and a temperate climate—and that they are inaccessible, protected from mundane incursions.

To the early American settlers in the eastern seaboard states, Kentucky seemed to substantially fit the description of a paradise on earth. It was shielded by a high wall of mountains to the east and river barriers on the north and south. The hunters who ventured into Kentucky in the 1750s and 1760s returned with reports of abundant game, fertile land, and an agreeable climate that only spurred on those seeking a rediscovered Eden.

The first account of Kentucky's climate appeared in a report prepared by the Jesuit Hierosme Lalemant covering the years 1661–62 and sent to his superior in France. Not having traveled to Kentucky himself, Lalemant relied on reports of Iroquois Indians who had raided the Shawnees there. His description established a mistaken concept of Kentucky climate that persisted for 150 years. He said of Kentucky: "It is a country which has none of the severity of our winters, but enjoys a climate that is always temperate—a continual spring and autumn, as it were." Similarly, an account published in Paris in 1821 by an unknown Frenchman described Kentucky as a region favored by a Côte d'Azur climate, one where snow rarely fell and, when it did, remained only a short time. But this account went one step further, making the equation with the rediscovered Eden explicit: "The air here is so pure, so serene almost all the year, that this country is veritably a second terrestrial paradise."

There were, however, somewhat earlier indigenous accounts. Gilbert Imlay, who owned and occupied a tract of land in Fayette County in addition to serving as land commissioner in the back settlements of Virginia, left Kentucky before the end of 1786, then published *A Topographical Description of the Western Territory of North America* in 1792. Imlay apparently did not dwell in the western country long enough to experience its weather extremes because his description speaks only of a remarkably delightful climate:

> You ascent [*sic*] a considerable distance from the shore of the Ohio, when you suppose you had arrived at the summit of a mountain, you find yourself upon an extensive level. Here an eternal verdure reigns, and the azure heavens, produces, in this prolific soil, an early maturity which is truly astonishing. Flowers full and perfect, as if they had been cultivated by the hand of a florist, and with all of the variegated charms which colour and nature can produce here in the lap of elegance and beauty, decorate the smiling groves. Soft zephyrs gently breathe on sweets, and the inhaled air gives a voluptuous glow of health and vigour, that seems to ravish the intoxicated senses. The sweet songsters of the forests appear to feel the influence of this gently [*sic*] clime, and, in more soft and modulated tones, warble their tender notes in unison with love and nature. Everything here gives delight; and in that mild effulgence which beams around us, we feel a glow of gratitude for the revelation which our all bountiful creator has bestowed upon us in the creation; but which has been contaminated by the base alloy of meanness, the concomitant of European education,

and what is more lamentable is, that is the consequence of your very laws and government.

The first hints that Kentucky had a semblance of winter appear in the writings of John Filson, who traveled to Kentucky with the early hunters and explorers, then chronicled their exploits, especially those of Daniel Boone. His *The Discovery, Settlement, and Present State of Kentucky*, which appeared in 1784, contained the following chapter, titled "Air and Climate":

> This country is more temperate and healthy than the other settled parts of America. In summer it wants the sandy heats which Virginia and Carolina experience and receives a fine air from its rivers. In winter, which at most only lasts 3 months, commonly 2, and is but seldom severe, the people are safe in bad houses and the beasts have a good supply without fodder. The winter begins about Christmas and ends about the first of March, at farthest does not exceed the middle of that month. Snow seldom falls deep or lasts long. The west winds often bring storms and the east winds clear the sky but there is no steady rule of weather in that respect as in the northern states. The west winds are sometimes cold and nitrous. The Ohio running in that direction and there being mountains on that quarter, the westerly winds by sweeping along their tops, in the cold regions of the air, and over a long tract of frozen water, collect cold in their course, and convey it over the Kentucky country; but the weather is not so intensely severe as the winds bring with them in Pennsylvania. The air and seasons depend very much on the wind, as to heat and cold, dryness and moisture.

The possibility of an extremely mild climate in Kentucky was a puzzle to residents of the Atlantic seaboard, who had become accustomed to occasional severe winter episodes even as far south as Virginia and the Carolinas. Lively arguments raged at scientific meetings for years. Thomas Jefferson never traveled more than 50 miles west of his home, Monticello, in central Virginia, but he constantly sought information about the country that his native state claimed west of the mountains. He questioned travelers about details of the climate and even proposed that every county in Virginia be provided with a thermometer to record temperatures so that an accurate study of climate differences could be conducted.

Jefferson believed that temperatures became colder as one moved west across Virginia and then warmer again after one crossed the mountains into Kentucky. He proposed his ideas in *Notes on the State of Virginia*, which was published in Philadelphia in 1788. According to Jefferson:

> In an extensive country, it will of course be expected that the climate is not the same in all its parts. It is remarkable that, proceeding on the same parallel of latitude westwardly, the climate becomes colder in like manner as when you proceed northwardly. This continues to be the case till you attain the summit of the Allegheny, which is the highest land between the ocean and the Mississippi. From thence, descending in the same latitude to the Mississippi, the change reverses; and, if we may believe travelers, it becomes warmer there than it is in the same latitude on the sea side. Their testimony is strengthened by the vegetables and animals which subsist and multiply there naturally, and do not on our sea coast. Thus Catalpas grow spontaneously on the Mississippi as far as the latitude of 37° and reeds as far as 38°. Perroquets even winter on the Sioto, in the 39th degree of latitude. In the summer of 1779, when the thermometer was at 90° at Monticello, and 96 at Williamsburg, it was 110° at Kaskaskia.

A Frenchman, Constantin François de Chasseboeuf, comte de Volney, visited the United States between 1795 and 1798, during which time he traveled from Washington, D.C., to Vincennes, Indiana. Volney had personal conversations with Jefferson about the climate of the Ohio Valley region, then returned to France and published his *View of the Climate and Soil of the United States of America*. In it he expanded on Jefferson's opinion: "The climate of the basin of the Ohio and of the Mississippi is less cold by three degrees of latitude than that of the Atlantic coast. . . . This is one of those singularities, that deserves so much the more attention, as I do not know that it has been described with all its circumstances." Volney's commentary cited the cultivation of cotton at Cincinnati and Vincennes as evidence of the softness of the climate. In order to explain the greater warmth claimed for the region, Volney postulated that there was a much greater prevalence of southerly winds in the Mississippi and Ohio Valleys than along the Atlantic seaboard, where he had often observed northeasterly winds dominating. This zonal difference was supposed to end at the Great Lakes because, north of that, Volney's evidence indicated, the interior of Canada was colder than the seaboard.

The ideas put forth by Jefferson and Volney were widely circulated in a young country eager to learn about itself. They were first refuted in 1810 by Dr. Daniel Drake, a Cincinnati physician and geographer. Drake's family had moved from New Jersey to Mays Lick, Kentucky, in 1788 when he was a small boy. In 1800, at age 15, Drake was sent to Cincinnati to begin studying medicine, and, throughout his medical career, he showed a keen interest in the effect of climate on health in the Ohio Valley. Drake published his *Notices concerning Cincinnati* in 1810. The book contained weather observations for the city over several years and also the statement:

From which it appears that the opinion concerning the greater heat of this climate first expressed by our late illustrious president, afterwards glanced at by Loskiel, and since supported and extended by Mr. Volney, is not at least, in its full extent correct. The former published his celebrated notes, at a time when but obscure accounts respecting this country had been received, the latter traveled here in 1796, and therefore should have possessed more correct information. He however, seems to have been sometimes misled by a favorite and ingenious, but not unexceptionable hypothesis.

During the early years of the nineteenth century, the medical and scientific communities in the United States were quite concerned with providing explanations of observed meteorological phenomena. Dr. Lewis Beck of the Albany Institute prepared a paper in 1823 dealing with the climate west of the Appalachians. It was entitled "An Examination of the Question, Whether the Climate of the Valley of the Mississippi under Similar Parallels of Latitude, Is Warmer Than That of the Atlantic Coast." And, in it, Beck cited more recent evidence that refuted Jefferson's and Volney's earlier conclusions.

If there was any controversy left, it was finally ended when *Climatology of the United States* was published by Lorin Blodget in 1857. Blodget wrote: "The early distinction between the Atlantic States and the Mississippi has been quite dropped, as the progress of observation has shown them to be essentially the same, or to differ only in unimportant particulars. The Ohio Valley at Cincinnati, the Atlantic Coast at Norfolk, and the interior of New York at Rochester, may each be swept over by some general change,—of pressure, temperature, winds, or rain,—and influenced as uniformly as if they were all located within a circuit of a hundred miles."

The early accounts might have been tempered somewhat if the writers had spent more time on the frontier. One of the most rigorous winters ever known to inhabitants of Kentucky occurred early in the state's history. Even though the settlers had no thermometers to record the exact degree of cold, the winter of 1779–80 must go on record as being one of the worst of all. Colonel William Fleming, who spent the winter at Fort Boonesboro on the Kentucky River, wrote in his diary on November 29, 1779: "It rained last night which was the first rain we have had since coming into this country. This night there fell a snow and so dark on the 29th that was bad traveling."

The weather turned cold the first week in December, with snow bringing an earlier winter than the settlers had apparently encountered during their short stay in Kentucky. On December 6, Fleming wrote: "Continued cold with snow. The inhabitants averred that they never knew so severe weather at that season the winter generally setting in about Christmas and continuing about 6 weeks." During the following weeks, the weather continued stormy but turned very cold on December 20, when Fleming noted: "The Kentucky has been full of ice for two days but was closed up this evening and frozen over." The river continued to freeze until, on December 29, horses with riders were able to cross it.

The first week in January brought more snow, with 12 inches on the ground on January 3. The hardships were becoming evident when Fleming made his entry for January 9: "The weather continued in the day clear and freezing in the night is severely cold as ever I felt it in America. The people at this place all sickly with colds. Two young men died yesterday. The frost had penetrated fourteen inches into the ground as we found by the opening of the graves." On January 19, he admitted: "So excessively cold we were afraid of being frostbit. The night violently cold." But it was not until January 24 that he wrote: "Crossed Kentucky on ice. . . . This day so exceeding cold I had one of my toes bit with frost and some of my fingers frozen." Fleming's next entry was not made until February 6, when he noted: "The frost still continuing, the Kentucky was frozen two feet thick of ice."

Stormy weather continued through February, but a gradual thaw developed about the middle of the month. Occasional snow and freezing temperatures occurred through March, however, and Fleming's entry for March 20 was a testimony to the severity of that winter season:

Last night it was cold and froze hard, the effects of the severe winter was now sensibly felt, the earth for so long a time being covered with snow and the water entirely froze, the caine [i.e., cane] almost all killed, the hogs that were in the country suffered greatly, being frozen to death in their beds. The deer likewise not being able to get either water or food were found dead in great numbers. Tirkies [sic] dropped dead off their roosts and even the buffaloes died starved to death. The vast increase of people, near three thousand that came into this country with the prodigious losses they had their cattle and horses, on their journey, and the severity of the winter after they got here killing such numbers, all contributed to raise the necessaries of life to a most extravagant price.

The winter that Colonel Fleming and his fellow frontiersmen

experienced can never be precisely compared to contemporary winters since, as we have seen, no actual temperature readings were made. The depth of the snow, the thickness of the ice, and the depth of the frost are, however, clues suggesting that it might rank among the three or four coldest winters since Kentucky was settled. Still, reports of that winter were not sufficient to turn away the families continuing to move west—seeking land in Kentucky, the earthly paradise.

OBSERVERS OF
KENTUCKY
WEATHER

An account of long-term weather trends in Kentucky depends on the store of knowledge that has been built up from meticulous and reliable daily observations made by hundreds of people over a period beginning more than 150 years ago. While rocks and fossils give clues to approximate climates, the observations written on paper provide some very specific information. The earliest recorded observations were likely made strictly out of curiosity about day-to-day weather variations or to reinforce a memory that is often too uncertain to win those frequent arguments about how cold, how hot, or how wet the weather was during a particular period. For the past 100 years, weather observing has been an acknowledged U.S. government function, with several agencies involved in collecting reports from both official and volunteer observers. No matter who took them, the observations collected over past years provide priceless information to be used in planning for the future.

For meteorological observations to be useful, the various weather elements must be measured under standard conditions. There are a number of observation locations in Kentucky that have been equipped with standard instruments that are calibrated and regularly inspected for accuracy. These are usually called *official* observing stations and are maintained by a government agency, university, or similar institution. Because of their quality, the records generated by these observing stations are usually included in the published climatic data for the state. Occasionally, reports indicating that records have been broken are received from individuals taking their own measurements (e.g., temperatures read on back porch thermometers), but only reports coming from standardized observing stations are considered to be official.

The exposure of the measuring instruments is very important if accurate readings are to be obtained. For example, temperature is measured with either a mercury or an electronic thermometer that is shielded from direct sunlight and open to the circulation of the wind. Care must also be taken to place the instrument well away from any buildings or sources of heat. The standard height at which temperature is measured is 5 feet (1.5 meters).

Rainfall is measured with an open gauge positioned at ground level. Accumulation is checked at least once each day. The standard rain gauge has an opening with a diameter of 8 inches or greater to obtain a representative measurement. Smaller sizes often undermeasure precipitation. A rain gauge cannot be obstructed by overhanging tree branches or nearby buildings. Some rain gauges are read manually with a simple ruler, while others have mechanical devices that measure the rainfall and also allow the rate of accumulation to be recorded.

For wind speed and direction to be accurately determined, measurements must be taken in a large open area in which the wind is unaffected by eddies or turbulence from nearby structures. Therefore, the most reliable wind data are compiled at airports, where the wind instruments, called *anemometers*, are usually placed alongside a runway. The standard height at which wind is measured is 33 feet (10 meters).

Other weather-observing equipment is sometimes installed for special purposes: for example, large open pans of water to measure the daily rate of evaporation or instruments to measure the intensity of sunshine. For agriculture interests, soil temperatures are important, and remote reading thermometers are used in some places to measure the temperatures below ground. The standard arrangement for measuring soil temperature uses a probe placed 4 inches beneath mowed grass in an open area. Sometimes an adjacent bare plot is also instrumented to obtain comparative readings.

Snowfall is one of the more difficult measurements to make. The snow falling in a rain gauge can be melted and the water content accurately measured, but the actual snow depth can be highly variable. Drifting can result in uneven depths, and observers must often average several different measurements to get a representative value.

An official weather-observing station does not necessarily have all types of measuring instruments present. Typically, there are more rain gauges placed in Kentucky than there are thermometers because there is greater variability in precipitation than there is in temperature. Whatever the instrument, the readings are regularly made by a government employee or volunteer observer and forwarded to the nearest National Weather Service (NWS) office.

Thermometers are among the most popular home weather instruments. However, early users of the instruments were little concerned with standardization of temperature readings. The concept of a device to measure the temperature was actually devised by Galileo Galilei in the early seventeenth century, but the mercury thermometer as we know it today was invented by Fahrenheit about 1714.

Thermometers were initially used mostly in laboratories in Europe. Few were found in the American colonies because they were costly and difficult to transport from England. The first person thought to have brought a thermometer to America was Cadwallader Colden, a physician who was born in Scotland. Colden settled in New York in 1718 and was named the first surveyor general of the colony. Later, lengthy series of meteorological observations were started at Charleston, South Carolina, by Dr. John Lining in 1737 and at Cambridge, Massachusetts, by Professor John Winthrop in 1742, both of whom owned thermometers. Benjamin Franklin possessed a thermometer as early as 1749.

Thomas Jefferson was an avid weather watcher who found time early in the morning of July 4, 1776, to buy a new thermometer, for which he paid £3 15s. He noted that the temperature was 68°F at 6:00 A.M. and had risen to 73.5°F by the time Congress sat down at 9:00 A.M. The highest temperature in Philadelphia that day was

76°F. Jefferson made daily entries in his garden book concerning temperature readings, which were taken as early as possible in the morning, then again at 4:00 P.M. He was, as we have seen, intensely interested in the nature of the western counties of Virginia, and, in November 1783, he purchased another thermometer and sent it to Ebenezer Zane, who lived in the western part of Virginia near the present site of Wheeling, West Virginia. Whether Zane received the thermometer is unknown, but no record of any readings made by him has ever been uncovered.

John Filson, who, as we have noted, wrote of early Kentucky explorers and settlers, purchased a thermometer to bring with him on a journey to the Kentucky area from Pittsburgh in May 1785. Filson's daily diary includes regular observations of sky condition, wind, and temperature, but apparently the thermometer was broken en route because precise temperature readings end midjourney, replaced by general descriptive terms.

It is not known how widely thermometers were used in pioneer Kentucky, but they did become available before 1800. An ad placed in the *Kentucky Gazette* of Lexington in 1796 listed assorted items available in a new shipment from the East, and thermometers were among them. The *Gazette*'s editor made occasional reference to local temperature readings in his news column whenever unseasonable weather occurred.

There is evidence that some type of regular temperature readings were being made at Transylvania University in Lexington soon after 1800. The *North American Review*, a journal of literature and culture, began publication in Boston in 1815, and, starting in its initial year, it contained temperature reports from a professor at Harvard and another from Bowdoin College. From June to August 1817, the publication included observations from a Professor Bishop at the "University in Lexington," which undoubtedly was Transylvania University. This was the first time in America that observations from geographically distinct locales were being collected and published.

The Shaker community established at South Union in Logan

County early in the nineteenth century was apparently very weather conscious. Residents' records include comments about daily weather conditions as early as 1806, but it was not until January 1819 that those records began to include specific temperature readings.

The initial weather observations by Professor Bishop were subsequently taken up by Professor Constantine Rafinesque, a renowned but controversial biologist who taught at Transylvania University. Rafinesque recorded the temperature at 7:00 A.M., noon, and sunset and also made notes about the progress of trees and shrubs and the appearance of animals. His observations appeared in print for the first time in the January 1820 issue of the *Western Review and Miscellaneous Magazine,* a frontier collection of literary and philosophical writings published in Lexington by William Gibbs Hunt from 1820 to 1824.

Rafinesque was known for his many but transient interests, and his reports appeared in Hunt's magazine only intermittently. But, not surprisingly, given the university's early emphasis on the natural sciences, another Transylvania faculty member, Thomas J. Mathews, the Morrison Professor of Mathematics and Natural Philosophy, showed a similar interest in the weather. Mathews's daily observations—made at 7:00 A.M., 1:00 P.M., and 7:00 P.M. and noting temperature, rainfall, pressure, wind, and other weather phenomena—appeared in print in February 1828 in the first issue of the *Transylvania Journal of Medicine and Associated Sciences.* A "Meteorological Journal" in the January 1828 issue also appears under his name.

The monthly reports appeared irregularly through 1837, various Transylvania faculty members apparently assuming responsibility for recording the weather. Dr. Lunsford P. Yandell took them for a part of that time. Yandell left his home in Tennessee to attend medical school at Transylvania, then returned to Tennessee to practice in Murfreesboro. He purchased a thermometer and began making readings with it. In 1835, he moved to Lexington as a professor of chemistry at Transylvania and brought his thermometer with him. While at the school he served for a time as the editor of the *Journal of Medicine* and is also credited with some of the weather observations appearing in it. About 1850, Yandell moved to Louisville to join the faculty of the new medical school being established there.

The U.S. Army started the first organized federal government program of weather observations. In 1818, Joseph Lovell, the army's surgeon general, ordered each army surgeon to "keep a diary of the weather" and to note "everything of importance relating to the medical topography of his station, the climate, diseases prevalent in the vicinity . . ." Assigning a weather-observation program to the army was logical. Army posts were widely distributed, reaching even into the frontier, and a range of observations could be collected among them. It is clear from the surgeon general's instructions that the climate was of particular interest because of its effects on disease.

In July 1825, the army surgeon at Newport Barracks in Kentucky began to record the temperature at sunrise, 2:00 P.M., and sunset and daily precipitation in inches and tenths. His remarks ranged widely and included comments on frost, dew, fog, thunder, lightning, gusty winds, and rises in the Ohio River. A copy of the first page of his weather observations is shown in figure 9.

The Newport reports frequently contained comments like the following from 1851: "It blew a hurricane at 1 P.M. During the space of 20 minutes there falling hail stones the size of chestnuts." Many entries were diary-like: "Tolerable pleasant today with occasional showers." Some recorded unusual events: "The Ohio River frozen over. Crossing on the ice." Some were terse: "Chilly"; "Rainy"; "Pleasant." Some were of necessity long: In January 1855, the average temperature was reported as 18.33°F. But the observation continued:

The average mean temperature for the month of January for 18 years was 31°. This has been the coldest month ever known here. On a few hours only during the month has the thermometer indicated a temperature above the freezing point. Snow has remained

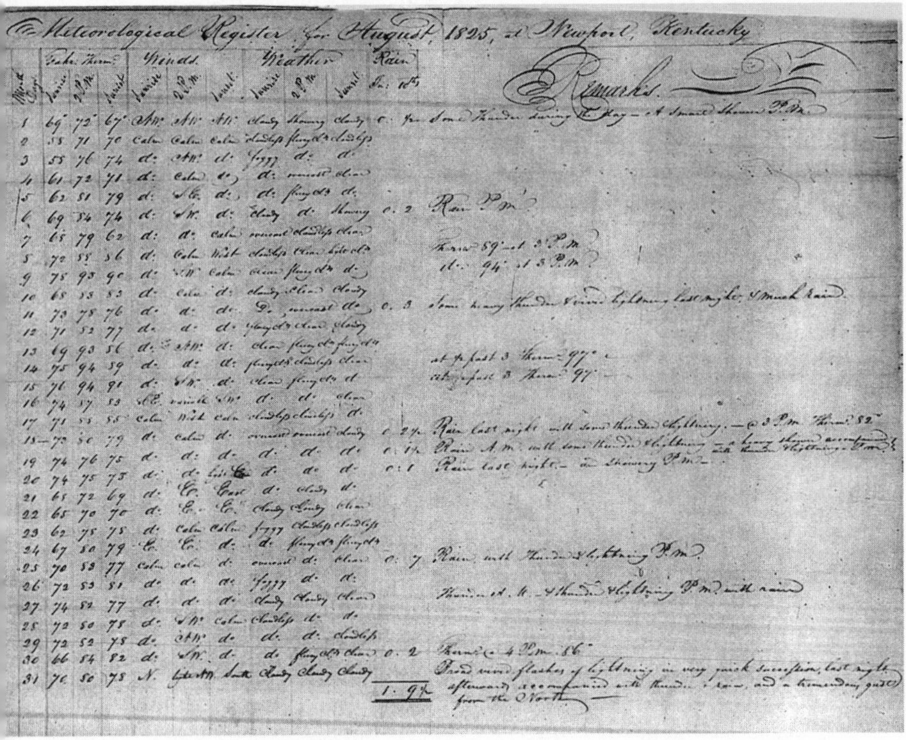

Meteorological Register for August, 1825, at Newport, Kentucky

Month Days	Fahr. Therm. Sunrise	Fahr. Therm. 2 P.M.	Fahr. Therm. Sunset	Winds Sunrise	Winds 2 P.M.	Winds Sunset	Weather Sunrise	Weather 2 P.M.	Weather Sunset	Rain In: 10ths	Remarks.
1	69°	72°	67°	NW	NW	NW	cloudy	showery	cloudy	0. [illegible]	Some Thunder during the Day – A Small Shower P.M.
2	58	71	70	Calm	Calm	Calm	cloudless	flying clds	cloudless		
3	55	76	74	do	NW	do	foggy	do	do		
4	61	72	71	do	Calm	do	do	overcast	clear		
5	62	81	79	do	SE	do	do	flying clds	do		
6	69	84	74	do	SW	do	cloudy	do	showery	0. 2	Rain P.M.
7	65	79	62	do	do	Calm	overcast	cloudless	clear		
8	72	88	86	do	Calm	West	cloudless	clear	light clds		Therm 89° at 3 P.M.
9	75	93	90	do	SW	Calm	clear	flying clds	do		do 94° at 3 P.M.
10	65	88	83	do	Calm	do	cloudy	clear	cloudy		
11	73	78	76	do	do	do	do	overcast	do	0. 3	Some heavy thunder & vivid lightning last night, & much rain.
12	71	82	77	do	do	do	flying clds	clear	cloudy		
13	69	93	86	do	NW	do	clear	flying clds	flying clds		
14	75	94	89	do	do	do	flying clds	cloudless	clear		at ½ past 3 Therm 97°
15	76	94	91	do	SW	do	clear	flying clds	do		at ½ past 3 Therm 97
16	74	87	83	SE	variable	SW	do	do	clear		
17	71	85	85	Calm	West	Calm	cloudless	cloudless	do		
18	72	80	79	do	Calm	do	overcast	overcast	cloudy	0. 24	Rain last night with some thunder & lightning. — @ 3 P.M. Therm 82°
19	74	76	75	do	do	do	do	do	do	0. 14	Rain A.M. with some thunder & lightning — a heavy shower accompanied with thunder & lightning P.M.
20	74	75	75	do	do	[illegible]	do	do	do	0. 1	Rain last night. — [illegible] showery P.M.
21	65	72	69	do	E.	East	do	cloudy	do		
22	65	70	70	do	E.	E.	cloudy	cloudy	clear		
23	62	75	75	do	Calm	Calm	foggy	cloudless	cloudless		
24	67	80	79	E.	E.	do	do	flying clds	flying clds		
25	70	83	77	Calm	calm	do	overcast	do	clear	0. 7	Rain with Thunder & lightning P.M.
26	72	83	81	do	do	do	foggy	do	do		Thunder A.M. – & thunder & lightning P.M. with rain
27	74	82	77	do	do	do	cloudy	cloudy	clear		
28	72	80	78	do	SW	Calm	cloudless	do	do		
29	72	82	78	do	NW	do	do	do	cloudless		
30	66	84	82	do	SW	do	do	flying clds	clear	0. 2	Therm @ 4 P.M. 86°
31	70	80	78	N.	[illegible]	South	cloudy	cloudy	cloudy	1. 94	Broad vivid flashes of lightning in very quick succession, last night afterwards accompanied with thunder & rain, and a tremendous gust from the North

FIGURE 9. *Newport Barracks weather record sheet (1825).*
(National Archives.)

upon the ground since the 25th of December 1854 with frequent accumulations. The River has been firmly closed since January 6, 1855 and the heaviest loaded crossed in safety. The atmosphere has been dry, pure, and bracing. Not a case of pneumonia or other inflammatory disease has occurred at the fort.

In Bowling Green, John Younglove, a pharmacist, kept his own meteorological records and made reference to specific temperatures as early as 1835. For that year he wrote: "The old people all over this region have for years spoken of the cold Friday that occurred on Friday, February 7th, 1835. The thermometer registered 18 degrees below zero. It had been cold the day before with considerable snow upon the ground, and what made it seem the colder was the wind blew a gale all day making it so disagreeable and cold that no one could remain out any length of time without freezing."

Another early weather observer in Kentucky was Laurence Young, who lived at Springdale, his farm just outside Louisville, near Anchorage. Although trained as a lawyer, Young was active as a horticulturist, founding the Kentucky Horticulture Society, and also served as the farm editor of the *Louisville Journal*. In 1842, he began making daily observations of the temperature and precipitation, keeping very detailed records. In 1849, he joined the network of weather observers being established across the country by Professor Joseph Henry, the secretary of the then-new Smithsonian Institution. For 30 years, until his death in 1872, Young continued as a volunteer weather observer in Kentucky. The record that he started continued to be kept by other observers in the Anchorage area for many years. The Smithsonian also established observers in several other Kentucky locations in the nineteenth century—at Blandville in Ballard County (1871–74), Nicholasville in Jessamine County (1861–63), Paris in Bourbon County (1855–59), and Danville in Boyle County (1853–97), the records in the latter kept by a Mr. O. Beaty—but none quite so early as that at Anchorage.

Various individuals who for one reason or another had a personal interest in the weather made observations at several other locations in Kentucky. Besides Mr. Younglove in Bowling Green, the Hillenmeyer family in Lexington began taking rainfall observations on their farm north of the city in 1858. Records also exist for Bardstown during the years 1858–61 even though the first official observing station was not established there until 1896. At Fort Thomas, observations were made from 1855 to 1876, then resumed again from 1889 to 1892.

Over the years, several attempts have been made to summarize the weather observations made in Kentucky and provide some insight into the long-term averages and extremes characteristic of the state. Richard Collins's *History of Kentucky*, published in 1874, contains a chapter discussing the climate of the state and detailing some of the various weather influences as well as oddities known to have occurred. Collins includes in that chapter the complete record of weather observations made by Laurence Young at Springdale as documentation. Collins's father had published the first *History of Kentucky* about 1840, and, when his son published the 1874 update of that work, the inclusion of Young's observations represented a valuable first attempt to document the state's weather.

Stephen Visher, a geography professor at Indiana University, wrote an excellent but little-known summary of Kentucky's climate in 1929. Visher had already written on the climate of Indiana and was subsequently hired by W. R. Jillson, the director of the Kentucky Geological Survey, to do a similar study for the Bluegrass State. The result was "The Climate of Kentucky," an excellent paper detailing the wealth of information collected over the years by Kentucky's weather observers, much of the data conveniently presented through maps and diagrams. Unfortunately, the paper was published along with four others in a collection whose title—*The Pleistocene of Northern Kentucky: A Regional Reconnaissance Study of the Physical Effects of Glaciation within the Commonwealth*—belies the wealth of weather data available in it.

Several other studies of Kentucky's climate have appeared since Visher's. In 1933, a series of booklets called the *Climatic Summary of the United States* was published by the U.S. Weather Bureau, one section covering western Kentucky and another eastern Kentucky, both authored by J. L. Kendall, who was in charge of the Louisville office of the Weather Bureau from 1919 to 1943. These sections included short discussions of climate features and many tables that were described as containing climatic information from all observing stations from the time of their establishment until 1930. Data were presented from twenty-two locations in western Kentucky and eighteen in eastern Kentucky. In 1941, the U.S. Department of Agriculture's yearbook—entitled *Climate and Man*—included separate chapters describing the climates of the forty-eight contiguous states. Another government report prepared in 1959 contains a few maps and tables along with a brief discussion by O. K. Anderson, head of the Louisville Weather Bureau office from 1949 to

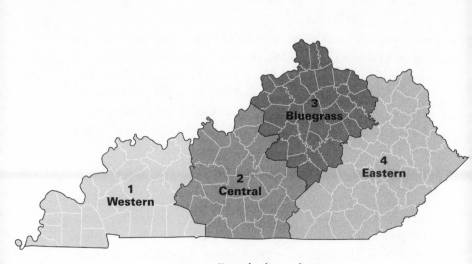

FIGURE 10. *Kentucky climate divisions.*
(Data provided by Kentucky Climate Center.)

1969. The last comprehensive study, my *Climate of Kentucky,* was published by the University of Kentucky Agricultural Experiment Station in 1976.

Responsibility for archiving and processing climate data in the United States now resides with the National Climatic Data Center, a part of the National Oceanic and Atmospheric Administration. The center collects data from many sources, such as government agencies, universities, and even research programs. Every 10 years, the center uses the observations to calculate new long-term averages, called *normals,* for each observing location. By convention, normals are the average for the most recent 30-year period. The last decade ended December 31, 2000, so the current normals are the averages for the period 1971–2000.

It has become convention in the United States to use averages for the most recent 30 years as a representative period for climate normals, rather than the entire record of observations, which can extend over 100 years or longer. These climate normals are often used to project the effects of weather on, for example, reservoirs, building design, or the demand for utilities over a period that can typically last 50–100 years. Some might think that, the longer the period of weather records taken into consideration, the more reliable the normals thus determined will be. However, there are trends in the weather data and changes that occur over periods shorter than 100 years. Climate change that shows up in the data can be either natural or man-made, but it must be filtered out. A shorter, recent sample will give a better estimate than a longer one. Therefore, using the most recent 30-year average to represent "normal" climate is believed to provide the best estimation of the average conditions that will occur during the following years.

The government weather agency has also used such observations to identify areas of the state that are as climatically homogeneous as possible. In Kentucky, there are four of these climatic divisions, and they are shown in figure 10.

TEMPERATURE

Kentucky's climate is characteristically referred to as *continental,* which implies that the region is located near the center of a large land area, away from the moderating influence of the sea. In the middle latitudes, where the state is located, this setting means that temperatures can cover a wide range over the course of a year. Not only do residents perspire under the extreme heat of the summer, but they can also sometimes shudder with the extreme cold of the winter.

Of all continental locations on earth, Siberia is the one in which we find the greatest variation in temperatures, the extremes there normally exhibiting a 140°F range between the warmest and the coldest temperatures. Fortunately, the range in Kentucky is only 95°F. Kentucky's temperature patterns can best be called *invigorating*—warm enough to provide an ample growing season, cold enough to provide the variety of a winter bracketed by prolonged spring and autumn periods.

Kentucky lies in a battleground of air masses where cold polar air and warm subtropical air alternately exert their influence. The greatest variations brought by these alternating air masses are apparent in January, when the average difference between maximum temperatures on successive days is about 8°F. This is shown in figure 11. Winter weather is more prone to great day-to-day fluctuations in Kentucky than in many other locations in the country. This explains the winter prevalence of sinusitis and similar health problems in the state.

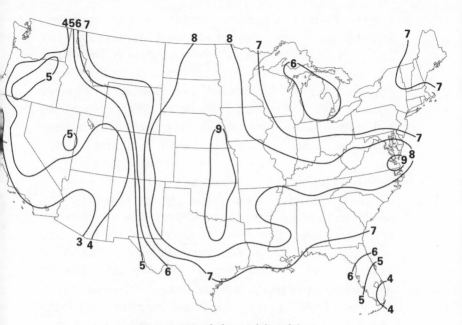

FIGURE 11. *Mean daily variability of the*
maximum temperature (°F) in January.
(Data provided by Department of Commerce.)

COLD

The extreme winter temperatures that affect Kentucky are usually caused by cold air masses that originate over the snow-covered regions of Siberia or the Canada-Alaska area, then move into the central United States. Early extreme readings of cold temperatures in Kentucky include -19.5°F at Louisville on January 1, 1864; -21°F at Transylvania University in Lexington on February 8, 1835; -30°F at Loretto on February 11, 1899; and -33°F at Sandy Hook that same date.

Every time the thermometer rises to an unseasonably high reading during the winter, there is an almost equal opportunity for it to drop rapidly to a very cold reading. These drastic changes—called *cold waves*—can easily result in the mercury dropping from around 70°F on an unseasonably warm winter day to 20°F the following morning. The modern Kentucky record for plunging temperatures was set in January 1963. After highs near 50°F on January 23, an arctic air mass invaded, producing frigid overnight lows. The temperature plummeted as much as 70°F in fourteen Kentucky cities. For example, a drop of 70°F was experienced at Benton, Golden Pond, and Richmond; 71°F at Heidelberg, Hopkinsville, and Somerset; 72°F at Bowling Green; 74°F at McKee; 75°F at Wolf Creek Dam; 76°F at Greensburg; and 81°F at Bonnieville. But the record setter that night was Bradfordsville, where the temperature dropped 82°F, from a high of 52°F to a low of -30°F.

Several frigid arctic air masses can move into Kentucky in succession during a lengthy period of cold weather, each having a progressively greater chilling effect. Many local records for the coldest temperature ever observed occurred during such an outbreak of arctic air in 1963, the beginning of which was heralded by the record plunging temperatures of January 23-24. On January 24, the first wave of cold air came through, and the mercury dipped to -34°F at Bonnieville in Hart County, which was sufficient to establish a new state record. Four days later, however, a second rush of arctic air arrived, and the Bonnieville record low was matched by a reading of -34°F at Cynthiana. Elsewhere in the state on that occasion, official records show temperatures of -33°F at Monticello, -22°F at Hopkinsville and Heidelberg, -21°F at Bowling Green and Lexington, and -20°F at Louisville and Frankfort.

The most severe modern cold wave occurred in 1994. In January, a blizzard coated the landscape with almost 1 inch of ice and topped it with anywhere from 6 to 26 inches of snow. Mason County had the heaviest snow accumulation. All state, interstate, and federal highways were closed for 2 days. Behind the blizzard came the intrusion of arctic air. This one brought frigid weather to all of Kentucky. The morning of January 19 saw -31°F at Grayson, -32°F at Somerset, -33°F at Cynthiana, and -35°F at Gray Hawk. But it was a reading of -37°F at Shelbyville that set the current official record for the lowest temperature ever observed in Kentucky.

Since Kentucky normally experiences wide variations in winter temperatures, one can find record high January readings almost as startling as the record lows. At most all locations in the state, the record high temperatures for January are well into the upper 70°s, and a few stations have observed readings in the low 80°s. At Loretto, the record high reading for the winter season was 83°F in January, a dramatic contrast to the –30°F record low there.

While the coldest temperatures of the year are usually noted during January, an unusually severe cold wave gripped Kentucky in February 1899. All across the Midwest temperatures were the coldest that they had been since 1872, and the weather brought extreme hardships. Schools and businesses were closed from February 10 to February 15. Trains were delayed or stalled because water was frozen and they were unable to get up steam. There was an unusually heavy demand for coal, which Kentucky mines were kept working overtime to fill. The roaring fires that people built to keep warm overtaxed stoves and chimneys and led to disastrous fires. Even the governor's mansion at Frankfort fell victim to one such fire; the governor and his family escaped uninjured, but the mansion was almost totally destroyed. No February before or since has had temperatures so cold, and, in a few Kentucky locations, the record lows set that month still stand. Official thermometers indicated –22°F at Maysville and –30°F at Vanceburg, while unofficial readings ranged down to –39°F at Cynthiana and Lebanon and a bone-chilling –42°F at Beaver Dam.

In some winter seasons, there is little variation in temperature, with the mercury remaining low for the entire period. For many years, the most severe winter season documented in the official weather records of Kentucky was the one that occurred during 1917–18, when the temperature for the 3-month period December–February averaged 28.6°F. Snow covered the ground in central Kentucky from late fall until spring. In December, the snowfall averaged 17.3 inches statewide. January was the coldest month on record to that time in much, if not all, of Kentucky. On January 12, temperatures of –12°F to –20°F at all except a few eastern stations, in combination with a wind speed of 30 mph, produced the most severe weather conditions in almost 20 years. The total snowfall for the month was the heaviest known to that date, some stations reporting more than 3 feet. There were numerous delays in business, including lengthy interruptions in tobacco sales because farmers were unable to deliver their crops.

That infamous cold winter opened on a note that was indicative of the weather to come. One of the fiercest blizzards to hit the state struck on December 9, 1917, with 16 inches of snow reported at Louisville in just 15 hours. The snow was whipped by 40-mph winds that piled it into drifts as high as 6 feet in Richmond, but all over the state trains and other traffic came to a near halt. The early cold caused the Ohio River to freeze over along its entire length, and ice was reported on the Mississippi River near Hickman. When the ice finally broke on January 30, the ice floes crushed more than a dozen steamboats and many smaller vessels, causing a loss of over $1 million.

The winter of 1976-77 came very close to replacing the winter of 1917-18 in the record books. For the 3-month period December-February, the temperature for the state averaged 28.8°F, which is only 0.2°F warmer than that record-holding winter. Still, January 1977 did succeed in replacing January 1918 as the coldest single month statewide for which weather records exist. For that entire month, temperatures averaged 18.4°F, with the coldest readings dropping to -25°F in Covington and Falmouth. That average temperature was equivalent to the normal January mark in Burlington, Vermont—a winter climate few Kentuckians are usually prepared to face.

That winter of 1976-77 was the first of three consecutive very cold winters that represented a marked contrast to several consecutive mild winters during the early 1970s. The second of the cold winters, 1977-78, finally broke the record set 60 years before for the coldest winter in modern Kentucky history. December 1977 was only moderately cold, averaging 2.5°F below normal, and, while January 1978 was very cold, at an average of 23.3°F, it was not as cold as the record-breaking January of the previous year. The factor that accounted for the winter record was the prolonged cold that lasted through February and caused that month's temperature to average 13.5°F below normal. When the 3-month period December 1977–February 1978 was averaged, the winter temperature worked out at 27.3°F, breaking the previous record by more than a degree.

The economic impact of the severe cold during these three winters was greater and more widespread than that of the 1917–18 season, not necessarily because of the inflated value of the losses, but because of the greater sensitivity of modern commerce to disruptive weather. For instance, by the early 1970s, many gas utility companies in Kentucky had reached the limit of their ability to service customers, and supplies were adequate only for the normal winter extremes. As widespread cold settled over most of the central and eastern United States early in January 1977, natural gas use soared, causing existing supplies to grow short. On January 4, the Columbia Gas Company announced a 40% curtailment that affected customers in a large area of central and eastern Kentucky. This was only the first indication of the impact that the cold would have on the state's residents.

Traffic on the Ohio River, which carries many of the winter essentials, such as heating fuel oil, road salt, and coal, was affected by the cold January as ice floes began to form and passage through the locks was slowed by ice and low water levels. By mid-January, river traffic was reduced by 50%–75%, and, on January 20, the Ohio was reported to be frozen bank to bank from Pittsburgh to near Paducah. Only the very largest towboats were attempting to batter through the ice, and heating fuel oil soon joined natural gas in short supply.

Frequent and heavy snowfall made it difficult to keep roads open, especially with supplies of road salt limited in some areas. The hazardous driving conditions faced by school buses, combined with a shortage of heat in classrooms, caused many public schools to be closed for extended periods. Some school systems placed employees on indefinite leave without pay. Even the number of blood donors dropped, and blood banks reported a sharp decline in their supplies.

It is, of course, not just transportation, but also utility service delivery that is affected by extremely cold winters. The lowest temperatures of the month occurred during the period January 17–19, with minimums reaching records at several locations. Temperatures as low as –25°F caused power lines to break, creating widespread power outages. Broken water lines were also common, the ground having frozen much deeper than usual under the onslaught of prolonged cold.

The loss in wages and commerce caused by an abnormally cold winter in modern Kentucky can only be estimated. The extremes of January 1977 were responsible for an assessed loss of $107.5 million to Kentucky agriculture alone. Nearly 100,000 cattle and calves were lost. Only approximate calculations can be offered of the costs to repair severe damage to highways; the loss of state revenues from income, sales, and coal severance taxes; or lost retail sales. The intangible costs of schools closed for nearly a month, the mental anguish of those unable to leave their homes for days, and other, similar hardships can never be calculated.

Sometimes cold weather can be caused by natural disasters occurring on such a large scale that they alter weather patterns. That was the case in 1816, generally referred to in weather history as "the year without a summer" or "eighteen-hundred-and-froze-to-death." The summer of 1816 saw abnormally cold temperatures, attributed by scientists to the Tambora volcano, which erupted on April 7, 1815, with such force that the Indonesian mountain was reduced in height from about 12,000 feet to 8,500. The resulting volcanic cloud lowered global temperatures by as much as 5°F. In New England, for example, frost occurred during each of the summer months in 1816. Debris was ejected high into the atmosphere in amounts almost ten times greater than during the famed 1883 Krakatoa eruption, also in Indonesia. The theory is that debris carried to such height and in such quantities would be spread worldwide by the winds and take a year or more to fall back to earth, in the meantime blocking appreciable amounts of sunlight and causing temperatures to fall.

An unusual amount of dust in the air over Lexington was, in fact, noted by the editor of the *Kentucky Gazette* in the May 13, 1816, issue: "Without rain for now about three weeks, the whole atmosphere is filled with a thick haze, the inconvenience of which is not diminished by the clouds of impalpable dust which floats in the air. The fields exhibit more of the aridity of autumn than of the freshness and verdure of spring." The best description of the weather in Kentucky during that infamous year was left by B. O. Gaines in his 1905 *History of Scott County*. Gaines described the succession of months as follows:

January was mild—so much so as to render fires almost needless in parlors.

December previous was very cold.

February was not very cold; with the exception of a few days mild like its predecessor.

March was cold and boisterous during the first part of it; the remainder was mild.

April began warm, but grew colder as the month advanced, and ended in snow and ice with a temperature more like winter than spring.

May was more remarkable for frown than her smiles. Buds and flowers were frozen; ice formed half an inch thick; corn was killed, and the fields were again and again planted until deemed too late.

June was the coldest ever known in this latitude. Frost, ice and snow were common. Almost every green thing was killed. Fruit was nearly all destroyed.

July was accompanied with frost and ice. On the 5th ice was formed the thickness of common window-glass.

August was more cheerless, if possible, than the summer months already passed. Ice was formed an inch thick. Corn was so frozen that the greater part of it was cut down and cured for fodder. Almost everything green was destroyed. Papers stated that it would be remembered by the present generations that the year 1816 was a year in which there was no summer. Very little corn ripened. Farmers supplied themselves from the corn produced in 1815 for the seed of the spring of 1817. It sold at from $4.00 to $5.00 per bushel.

September furnished about two weeks of the mildest weather of the season. Soon after the middle it became very cold and frosty and ice formed a quarter of an inch thick.

October produced more than its share of cold weather—frost and ice abundantly.

November was cold and blustery. Enough snow fell to make good sleighing.

December was quite mild and comfortable.

HEAT

In contrast to the observed variety in the severity of Kentucky winters, the summer season does not normally have extreme and erratic variations. Generally, temperatures warm into the mild 70°F range by the middle of spring and remain warm through October. Average daytime high temperatures range from the mid- to the upper 80°s during the middle of the summer, but readings in the 90°s are not uncommon. In the extreme southwestern counties, the mercury reaches or exceeds 90°F on 50 or more days during an average year. The same occurs on about 40–50 days in the central sections. The east has even fewer hot days, with temperatures in the area from Lexington east usually rising above 90°F on 25 or fewer days per year.

Record high temperatures coincide with periods of very dry weather since cloudless skies and dry soil allow the sunshine to have the maximum heating effect. The summer of 1930, when Kentucky suffered the most severe drought in its history, was also a summer of extreme heat. A state temperature record was set at Greensburg on July 28, 1930, when the mercury officially reached 114°F. Among the other high temperatures that day were 113°F at Bowling Green, 112°F at Bardstown, Lovelaceville, and Middlesboro, and 111°F at Anchorage and Franklin. The heat wave continued through August 9, bringing Lovelaceville's total days above 100°F to 30. The highest unofficial reading was 117°F at Hickman in 1930. Extremes that have been noted at official weather stations elsewhere in the state then or at other times are given in appendix table A3.

During the summer of 1930, the weather was notable for the discomfort that it brought. The extreme heat was responsible for numerous deaths from heat prostration, including nine in Louisville and two in Covington. Many drownings occurred as people searched out any creek, river, or pond for relief from the oppressive temperatures. One Lexington farmer shot himself in despair after seeing the condition of his crops during this period of searing heat and prolonged dryness. He left a suicide note that said: "I would rather be dead than see my family suffer which I will have to see if the weather don't change so I will put an end to my troubles and end it."

The summer of 1936 was another period of record-breaking heat in Kentucky and goes into the books as being the warmest summer season on record. In Louisville, the average temperature from June through August was 81.0°F, almost 5°F above the 76.5°F normal for that 3-month period. Another heat wave occurred in 1952, and what it lacked in intensity, it made up for in duration. Princeton experienced 35 consecutive days with temperatures of 90°F or higher. The final 90°F reading of the year there occurred on October 1 and brought the year's total to an incredible 95 days of 90°F or higher. However, residents of Hopkinsville could argue that their 14 consecutive days at or above 100°F from August 27 through September 9 should be considered the hottest of the hot.

Very warm weather has been noted in Kentucky as early as April. For example, the mercury reached 90°F at Louisville on April 17, 1896. And the earliest 100°F reading there came on June 3, 1895.

Kentucky summers often combine high temperatures with high humidity, making the weather not just oppressive but downright dangerous. In 1999, excessive heat and humidity during the latter half of July took a toll on the unprepared. Before it was over, some 232 deaths were attributed to the heat throughout the Midwest. In Hopkinsville, Kentucky, a 75-year-old man died of hyperthermia; the single window air conditioner in his house was inoperative and all the windows closed (some even boarded up), allowing the indoor temperature to reach 120°F. The unrelenting heat triggered all-time peak-usage records at several Kentucky utilities, including the Paducah and Owensboro power systems. Some minor related outages were reported. The weather increased heat-related hospital visits, primarily for heat exhaustion. Shelters were opened at a few locations, and charities distributed free fans to the needy. Western Kentucky was under a heat advisory for over a week. High temperatures reached 100°F at Paducah on July 29 and 30, with afternoon heat indices commonly in the 110°F–115°F range. This was the fifth-warmest July on record at Paducah.

FROST AND FREEZE

The period when temperatures normally remain above 32°F is referred to as the *growing season,* although there are several freeze-tolerant vegetables that are not damaged by temperatures below 32°F. In Kentucky, the length of the growing season usually ranges from about 200 days in the western counties to 180 days in the central sections and 170 days in the northeast. There can, however, be quite a bit of variability in the length of the growing season. In one year out of ten it can be as long as 230 days in western Kentucky or as short as 150 days in eastern Kentucky.

The average date of the last freeze in the spring (at the standard thermometer height of 5 feet) ranges from April 5 in western Kentucky to May 1 in eastern Kentucky. In other words, the last freeze will occur after the average date in one year out of two. And it is only about 3 weeks after the average date that the risk of a freeze approaches zero. If 36°F is used as the threshold for the risk of frost damage, the last freeze will occur 10–15 days later than if the 32°F threshold is used.

The average date of the first freeze in the fall ranges from about October 12 in the east to about October 30 in the southwest. But freezing temperatures have been reported as early as September 9 in northern Kentucky. In 1975, the growing season extended long into the fall, the first widespread freeze occurring only on November 14.

At the other extreme, a killing frost has occurred in Kentucky before the end of August. In an 1842 interview, Jesse Graddy, who had come to Woodford County in 1788, reported: "The second year I came, the frost came on the 28th day of August, 1789, I think, 53 years ago, and bit all the corn that wasn't very forward. There was scarcely any good corn in the country. After that except some old corn (last year's crop)."

One of the longest growing seasons on record occurred in 1922. At Lexington, 243 days elapsed between the last spring freeze on March 22 and the first fall freeze on November 20. Near Wickliff the same year, 253 days passed during the freeze-free period.

SOIL TEMPERATURE

An important feature of Kentucky's climate is the usual extremes noted in the soil temperature, which behaves similarly, but not identically, to the air temperature. Most plants have minimum temperatures below which seed will not germinate and the plant will not grow; consequently, knowledge of soil temperature can be very useful for agricultural and horticultural planning. Although the time when the soil reaches a certain critical temperature varies somewhat from year to year, that annual cycle is usually relatively consistent. Heavy rains and wet soils can delay warming in the spring, but the time when average temperatures reach 50°F or 60°F usually will not vary by more than a few weeks. The average annual soil temperature ranges from 64°F at Mayfield to 57°F at Flemingsburg.

Even though average temperatures at 4 inches below sod remain above freezing throughout the year, there are brief periods during the winter when the upper layer will freeze. Bare soil will also occasionally freeze to depths greater than 4 inches. The depth to which soil freezes can be important in determining how deep to place water pipes or underground equipment to minimize the risk of freeze damage. The maximum depth to which bare ground has been noted to freeze solid ranges from 5 inches in southwestern Kentucky to 10 inches in the northeast.

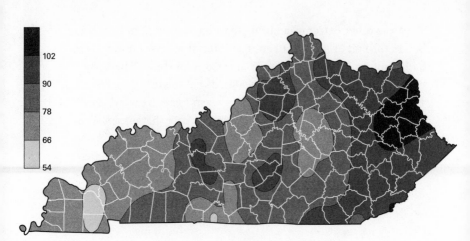

FIGURE 12. *Average number of freeze-thaw
events in Kentucky per year, 1966–95.
(Data provided by Kentucky Climate Center.)*

During the winter season, the soils in Kentucky experience
many freeze-thaw cycles that consist of sequences when the moisture in the soil alternately freezes and melts. This causes alternate
expansion and shrinkage of the soils and damages roads and foun-
dations. Since, as we have seen, Kentucky lies in a battleground of
cold and warm air masses, the economic impact of the freeze-
thaw cycles can be severe. Studies by the Kentucky Climate Center
using temperature data from 1966 to 1995 have determined that,
across the state, the number of these cycles ranges from fifty to
one hundred per year, with the greatest number occurring in the
eastern quarter of the state. The distribution is shown on the map
in figure 12.

6

RAIN, SNOW,
AND ICE

What preoccupation with the weather would cause Kentucky folklore to be filled with sayings such as "When a chicken oils its feathers, you can expect rain," "Expect rain when a cat washes its face around its ear," or "When fire spits, there will be snow"? Obviously, these and hundreds of similar sayings are characteristic of people who find their daily lives influenced by the presence or absence of precipitation. In Kentucky's normal climatic state, precipitation is regular and disruptive, but those who come to depend on its regularity are often frustrated.

PRECIPITATION
The low-pressure systems and their attendant cold or warm fronts that move through Kentucky during the colder months of the year are responsible for ample amounts of precipitation. In the summer, it is mainly the occasional shower or thunderstorm that brings precipitation. As a result of these seasonal factors, precipitation in Kentucky is well distributed. The state does not have what many other parts of the world have come to know as a definite and predictable dry season. On average, the driest month is October, when rainfall amounts average about 2–3 inches.

Precipitation in Kentucky is relatively evenly distributed throughout the year, and the yearly total is generally in the range of 45–50 inches. Monthly averages for four locations across the state are shown in figure 13. Such long-term averages do not, however, indicate the extremes that can occur. On rare occasions,

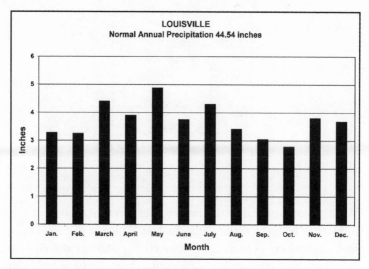

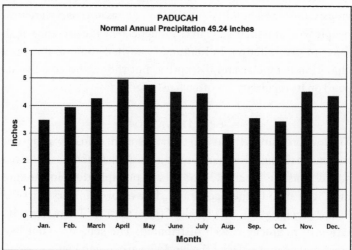

FIGURE 13A. *Monthly precipitation distribution*
bar charts, Louisville and Paducah.
(Data provided by National Climatic Data Center.)

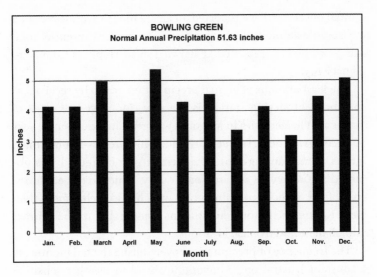

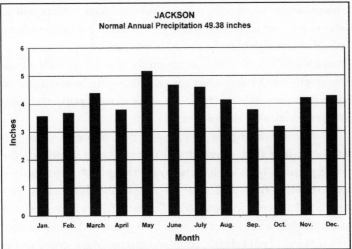

FIGURE 13B. *Monthly precipitation distribution
bar charts, Bowling Green and Jackson.
(Data provided by National Climatic Data Center.)*

rainfall observers have reported an entire month with less than a measurable amount of precipitation. The greatest monthly total was 22.97 inches, reported at Earlington in Hopkins County in January 1937.

The least amount of annual precipitation normally received at an official observing station is the 1971–2000 average of 38.38 inches at Wheelersburg in Magoffin County. The driest single year on record was observed at Mayfield, which received only 19.26 inches of rain during 1901. The wettest year on record was observed at Caneyville in Grayson County, which received an incredible 88.07 inches of rain in 1979, roughly 40 inches more than most Kentucky stations, an amount comparable to the normal rainfall in humid tropical locations.

The frequency of precipitation, even during the fall months, is a constant frustration to anyone involved in weather-sensitive outdoor work. On average, at any particular location there will be about 10–12 days with measurable precipitation each month from December through May. Summer showers are somewhat less frequent but can be expected to occur on about 6–8 days each month from August to October. Over the year, there will be about 105–10 days with measurable precipitation in the western portion of Kentucky, 125–45 days in the eastern.

Total rainfall during the growing season is, of course, an important factor in a state's agricultural potential. For Kentucky, the growing season is, as we have seen, the roughly 180–200-day period extending from mid-April to late October in the west and from late April to mid-October in the east. Total average rainfall for that period is 20–25 inches, which is typical of the midwestern United States. That rainfall, coupled with moisture stored in the soil the previous winter, works to produce Kentucky's usually abundant crops.

As noted earlier, however, precipitation is not always as regular as Kentuckians would like it to be. In fact, extreme variability from the average characterizes Kentucky rainfall. The state's summer showers are well known for their ability to produce excessive amounts of rainfall in a very short period. Data on rainfall amounts collected via rain gauges equipped with recorders able to measure intervals as short as 5 minutes indicate that the maximum 12-hour rainfall in the state was 9.68 inches at Scottsville on June 23, 1969, when south-central Kentucky and north-central Tennessee were pounded by thunderstorms. In Allen County, Kentucky, Trammel Creek flooded so severely that it claimed three lives and damaged a hundred homes, and the rain damaged 50% of all crops. All told, the storms caused $28.5 million in damage countywide. Across the state line in Red Boiling Springs, Tennessee, flooding caused approximately $2 million in damage and resulted in the deaths of two young children in the swollen Salt Lick Creek.

The greatest rainfall in Kentucky during a calendar day was 10.40 inches, recorded on June 28, 1960, at Dunmor in Muhlenberg County. That rain fell while Lake Malone was under construction, and water backing up behind the dam completely covered two earth movers, a bulldozer, and a great deal of other equipment to a depth of 20 feet. The greatest rainfall for any 24-hour period was 10.48 inches, recorded in Louisville between February 28 and March 1, 1997.

Many of the extremely heavy rainfall events occur during the warm months, when the air is able to hold the greatest amount of moisture. Showers occur when a warm, moist air mass rises and cools. While some showers develop when a cold front or a low-pressure system moves through a region and lifts the air, most summer rainfall is the result of the air being lifted by daytime heating of the ground. As a result, summer precipitation in Kentucky shows a distinct tendency to fall in the afternoon and early evening hours. There is a minimum of rainfall between sunset and noon.

Most of the greatest monthly precipitation records were the result of a series of heavy rainfall events rather than just one. The most dramatic example of a series of heavy storms occurred in January 1937. During that month, Kentucky's statewide precipitation totals averaged 15.77 inches—over four times the normal average of 3.77 inches. Of fifty-one stations in the central and western regions, forty-five had more than 15 inches, twelve had more than

20 inches, and Earlington in Hopkins County established a new monthly record of 22.97 inches. Almost all the precipitation was rainfall rather than snowfall, and 8 days of the month even saw thunderstorms. The result of this excessive rainfall was what has become known as the Great Flood of 1937. Over half of Frankfort and Louisville, and 95% of Paducah, was inundated. Mass evacuations from those cities and others along the Ohio River occurred. The Kentucky, Green, and Barren Rivers, as well as other rivers and creeks in central and western Kentucky, reported major flooding.

Some of Kentucky's heaviest rainfalls can be caused by remnants of tropical cyclones that reach the state as small, strong low-pressure systems. These systems start off as hurricanes or tropical storms, but they usually lose the strong winds developed over the ocean after they cross the U.S. coastline. They still have the potential to pack a major wallop, however, bringing with them heavy and prolonged rains and sometimes gusty winds and even isolated tornadoes.

Tropical storms that cross the central or western Gulf Coast will often move north and curve across the Ohio Valley as they move toward the northeastern United States. Others that cross the eastern Gulf Coast or the Atlantic seaboard will sometimes move north across the Appalachian Mountains, where the potential exists for extensive flooding. In the United States, there are sometimes ten to twelve tropical cyclones that threaten or reach the mainland annually, but numbers can vary greatly year by year. In not all years will the remnants of tropical storms reach Kentucky.

In September 1965, Hurricane Betsy struck the Texas coast and continued to move into the Ohio Valley, where it brought rainfall amounts up to 5 inches over portions of Kentucky. A major disaster occurred in the Appalachian region of Virginia in 1969 when Hurricane Camille moved inland across Mississippi and brought excessive rainfall along with it. The eastern counties of Kentucky received about 2–4 inches of rain from the storm, but the headwaters of the James River in Virginia saw torrential downpours of 12–20 inches in 24 hours, causing record flooding and over a hundred deaths.

The summer of 1979 was particularly busy for Kentucky, three separate tropical storm systems moving across the state. Hurricane Bob had diminished from hurricane to tropical storm intensity when it crossed the Louisiana coast in mid-July and headed directly for Kentucky. The storm passed over the western part of the state, then turned east through the Ohio River valley, heading toward West Virginia. In early September, Hurricane David moved up the east coast of Florida and headed north toward the Appalachian Mountains. Before making landfall in the United States, David had been an extremely intense hurricane, with winds of 170 mph. When it crossed Virginia, it brought especially heavy rainfall to the Appalachian Plateau. Heavy rains caused by the storm extended from eastern Kentucky to the Atlantic seaboard, where it spawned tornadoes and damaging winds. Hurricane Frederic, which came ashore near Mobile and headed northeast, crossed eastern Kentucky on September 13 and 14. It too was responsible for heavy rains and flooding, but, because it was moving very fast, it resulted in little damage.

On September 27, 2002, the remnants of Tropical Storm Isidore moved north from the Gulf Coast as a tropical depression, causing over 6 inches of rain within 24 hours in central Kentucky and around the Louisville area. Minor flooding occurred, but, in this case, the storm brought beneficial rain to some locations that had been experiencing a prolonged period of dryness. On the evening when Isidore's hardest rains were moving across the state, the University of Louisville's football team was playing a home game against powerful Florida State University, which held the nation's number four ranking. The driving rains made play difficult for both teams, but the Louisville Cardinals finally upset their opponents in overtime by a score of 26 to 20.

In 2004, the southeastern United States had a particularly busy tropical storm season, with four named storms striking Florida. Two of those moved north to cause heavy rain in Kentucky. They were particularly notable because they arrived in close succession.

Hurricane Frances struck Florida on September 5 and moved north, causing heavy rain a few days later over the Carolinas and eastern seaboard. This rain extended west into Kentucky on September 8 and 9. Rainfall for the two days ranged between 4 and 6 inches in many places in the eastern portion of the state. There was extensive local flooding, and many roads were closed, but no serious damage or loss of life was reported.

Less than 2 weeks later, Hurricane Ivan struck the Florida Panhandle, making landfall on September 16, and moving north to bring 2 days of heavy rain to eastern Kentucky starting on September 17. Rainfall totals measured for the storm were up to 5 inches, and this caused many streams to leave their banks. Local flooding occurred, and many roads were closed. Most of the major streams in eastern Kentucky and extending into the Bluegrass region reached flood stage, but no major losses were reported. More extensive flooding occurred on the upper reaches of the Ohio River, but this affected mostly West Virginia and Ohio.

Precipitation variability can have a significant impact in a state such as Kentucky where agriculture and urban development have become established in anticipation of regular and adequate rainfall but rainfall totals are, in fact, highly variable. For example, the normal July total at Bowling Green is 4.08 inches, but in one year out of ten the rainfall can be expected to total less than 1.73 inches, and in one year out of ten it will exceed 7.96 inches. Several consecutive weeks or even months of light rainfall, especially during the summer, can cause limited crop damage and water supply shortages. Such dry spells occur occasionally in many sections of the country, but the term *drought* is reserved for periods of moisture deficiency that are relatively extensive in both time and area.

The precipitation extremes that are observed in Kentucky are a pointed reminder that weather is never "normal." It is a series of extremes. Those who plan on the long-term average or normal precipitation amounts will usually find their cup either running over or nearly empty instead of manageably full.

SNOW

During the colder months of the year, a portion of Kentucky's precipitation is received in the form of snow, ice, or sleet rather than rain. For most of the state, snowfall amounts are usually limited, contributing to no more than 5% of the total moisture received during the year. Mean annual snowfall ranges from about 5 inches in the extreme southwestern counties to about 25 inches in the northeastern counties. In the higher elevations of eastern Kentucky, however, average snowfall amounts can be expected to be somewhat greater. The colder temperatures on Pine Mountain and Black Mountain allow a greater portion of the winter precipitation to fall as snow, rather than rain, and the average snowfall on the ridges is about 40 inches per year.

Even though snowfall is normally minimal in Kentucky compared to that received by its neighbors to the north, some winter storms can produce it in abundant amounts. During the 4-day period March 7–10, 1960, a winter storm dropped 27 inches of snow on Bowling Green. March 9 even saw a 24-hour record there of 18 inches. The storm also dropped 13 inches of snow on Lexington, where many Bowling Green residents had come to see Western Kentucky University play Miami of Florida in the NCAA basketball tournament. Five busloads of students returning home to Bowling Green after the game were stranded in the drifts near Munfordville for hours until they were finally rescued by a Louisville and Nashville Railroad (L&N) passenger train dispatched as an emergency measure by Governor Combs.

Blizzards are by far the most dangerous of all winter storms. They are characterized by temperatures below 20°F and winds of at least 35 mph, and they must also have enough falling or blowing snow to reduce visibility to 0.25 mile or less for at least 3 hours.

In mid-March 1993, a major blizzard struck parts of Kentucky. From March 12 to March 15, the eastern United States was ravaged by what some call "the storm of the century." Early in the week beginning Monday, March 9, the sophisticated computer models employed by the National Weather Service had forecast that a severe winter storm would be forming from a major cluster of thunderstorms in the Gulf of Mexico. A few days later, weather maps showed that the storm had formed and grown significantly. By Thursday, March 12, it was barreling up Florida's west coast with high winds, tornadoes, and a storm surge 12 feet above normal. The next day, it was carving a destructive path through the southeastern states, leaving eastern Kentucky paralyzed.

The blizzard of March 1993 was one of the largest winter storms in terms of snowfall and size in Kentucky history. Previously, the modern record for a single day's snowfall in the state had been 18 inches, but this storm broke that record at more than one station in eastern parts of the state. For example, 24 inches fell in Ashland on March 14. By the time the storm was over, most of eastern and southeastern Kentucky was covered with up to 30 inches of snow. There was 20 inches of snow on the ground in Jackson and Closplint, 22 inches in London, and 30 inches in Perry County, the most in Kentucky. Of course, the Perry County total pales in comparison with the 56 inches on Mount Leconte in Tennessee.

Along with the snow came brutal winds. Wind speeds up to 43 mph were recorded in Pike County, and a 30-mph clip blew over much of the state, creating large snowdrifts (8–10 feet in many places) and making the cleanup effort extremely difficult. I-75 from Lexington to the Tennessee border was shut down for two days, as was I-64 from Lexington east. All state and federal highways south of I-64 and east of I-75 were also closed. Over four thousand motorists were left stranded. Emergency shelters were established throughout much of eastern Kentucky. Many people found themselves sleeping in high school gyms or other public facilities. The National Guard had to be brought in to aid in rescue efforts, to clear roads, and to open twenty armories as additional shelters.

During the storm, 30 counties were forced to close schools and government offices. Of Kentucky's 120 counties, 73 were designated as eligible for reimbursement for the cost of emergency snow removal. The massive March 1993 blizzard was responsible for five deaths in Kentucky and over 270 nationwide. For the first time, every major airport along the East Coast was closed at some point because of the storm. With damage costs exceeding $1.6 billion, the blizzard of 1993 is ranked as the fourth-costliest storm in U.S. history.

The winter of 1977–78 produced duration records. Snow covered Kentucky for long periods that season, with most January and February days reporting some amount on the ground. On each of the 28 days of that February, sixty-five of eighty-nine reporting stations measured 1 inch or more on the ground. None compared to Williamstown in Grant County, however, where, beginning on January 8, 1978, 74 consecutive days with a trace or more of snow on the ground were reported.

On January 20, 1978, La Grange in Oldham County measured a snow depth of 31 inches. Not quite as deep, but still memorable, was the April 1987 snowfall. By dawn on April 3, snow had accumulated to a depth of 4 inches at Freeburn in Pike County. Snowfall continued there for the next two days until it reached its greatest depth of 28 inches on April 5. Gusty winds accompanied the snow, and snowdrifts 10 feet high were reported in Letcher County. Melting from the rapid warming that followed resulted in severe flash flooding in Letcher and Pike Counties. The heaviest snowfall for any month in Kentucky is the 46.5 inches recorded at Benham in March 1960. Over the entire 1959–60 winter season, Benham received 108.2 inches of snow.

Ample snowfall can occur during any of the winter months, but, interestingly, at most locations in Kentucky, the heaviest snows have fallen in March. This is because the ability of the air to hold moisture changes with temperature. During the cold month of January, the air can hold only a limited amount of moisture and, thus, produce only a limited amount of snow. As temperatures warm through February and March, the air is able to hold more and more moisture and, thus, produce more and more snow. In most instances of heavy snowfalls, temperatures are very close to the freezing mark, and the snow takes the form of large fluffy flakes that accumulate in a heavy wet snowpack, the weight of which can cause awnings and even roofs to buckle.

Snow seldom stays on the ground long in Kentucky. Brief warm periods develop even in midwinter, causing the snow to melt within a few days. On average, snow covers the ground to a depth of 1 inch or more at any particular location on only 10 days each year in the western part of the state and 15–20 days in the eastern. Of course, in the higher elevations of eastern Kentucky, snow cover can be expected to last somewhat longer.

Near the end of each year, as the holiday season approaches, most people look forward to a white Christmas. A review of the weather records for a representative period of 30 years between 1961 and 1990 reveals, however, that the chances of having a white Christmas in Kentucky are not good. The probability that there will be 1 inch or more of snow on the ground on Christmas Day is about 5%–10% in the western half of the state and 10%–25% in the eastern.

Snow usually makes its first appearance in Kentucky during the month of November, and measurable amounts often occur as late as April. There have, however, been cases of significant snows earlier and later. In October 1925, temperatures averaged much colder than normal, and 5–6 inches of snow accumulated at several locations, one sign that an early winter was on its way. In May 1894, 6 inches of snow accumulated at Lexington, among other places.

The peculiarities of that heavy snow were recorded by Mrs. Maggie Bailey, who lived about 50 miles east of Lexington. Her account was reprinted in the "Town Pump" column of the Bath County newspaper on May 20, 1976:

> The snow is six inches deep and is still snowing at 10 o'clock, Sunday, May 20th, 1894. The trees are in full leaf and are bending to the ground with the weight of the snow. Some of them are broken down the snow is so heavy.
>
> The blackberries are in bloom, but they are bent down to the ground with the snow. The locusts are in bloom.
>
> My peas are in bloom and beans are six inches high to say nothing of onions, radishes, and lettuce which we have had to eat for two weeks.
>
> I have 120 chickens and 27 turkeys and I don't know what to do with them. It is the lonesomest-looking time. The wheat is heading out and the corn is five or six inches high. Tobacco plants are ready to set out.

The snow did not melt off as soon as would be expected. It lay on the ground all day Monday. Then we had frost for about a week which killed all the fruits and vegetables.

ICE

While snowstorms can be inconvenient and dangerous, occasionally a set of conditions can develop that produces one of the most devastating of nature's menaces—the icestorm. When temperatures close to the ground and the temperature of the ground itself happen to be below freezing but the air overhead is above freezing, rain can fall and form a glaze on exposed objects. Prolonged heavy freezing rain coats everything with a thick layer of ice. Ice on the streets and sidewalks brings transportation to a standstill. But the weight of ice is even more dangerous. An ice coating 3 inches in diameter on telephone wire weighs about 1 pound per foot, and it has been estimated that an evergreen tree 50 feet high and 20 feet wide can be coated with as much as 5 tons of ice. No wonder, then, that ice can bring down utility lines and even utility poles.

A severe icestorm can throw a modern urban community into chaos. Witness the icestorm that struck Lexington on Christmas Day 1890. It brought down electric lines, cutting off power. The city's recently electrified trolleys were forced out of service, and the trolley company considered resurrecting its old horse-drawn cars, but the many power lines down across the tracks meant that nothing could run on them. The storm also brought down telephone and telegraph lines—and all the Western Union telegraph poles between Lexington and nearby Richmond—cutting off communications. Power was off for 5 days in Lexington, and the city's newspapers were estimating that it would be February before service was restored to outlying areas.

The effects of most icestorms are transient, freezing rain falling for only a brief period before warmer temperatures set in, and any ice that forms melting quickly. A much more serious situation occurs whenever temperatures drop after ice has accumulated and remain below freezing for several days. This is precisely what caused one of the most severe icestorms ever seen in Kentucky, that which struck statewide in the winter of 1951.

Late in the month, an unusually strong high-pressure system began pulling cold polar air into the region. Meanwhile, as a strong low-pressure system moved along a cold front that stretched from the Gulf of Mexico toward the Northeast, sleet and freezing rain spread over much of the South beginning on January 31. A weather-balloon reading from Nashville, Tennessee, at 9:00 P.M. the day before had indicated that temperatures at the surface were well below freezing—about -8°C (18°F)—and that there was a northeast wind. However, at just 5,000 feet above the surface, winds were from the southwest, and the temperature was well above freezing—closer to 9°C (48°F). This set up a perfect environment for freezing rain to develop.

On the morning of January 31, nearly 3 inches of snow and sleet had covered Bowling Green. Traffic was at a standstill. By noon, the snow had turned to rain as warm air aloft had moved over the region. But, with the surface temperature standing at 28°F, the rain froze on impact. Bulldozers were used in an effort to scrape the ice off the roads, but they made little headway. By the afternoon, the temperature had warmed just enough to turn some of the ice to slush, a sign that the situation might be improving.

Instead, conditions worsened the next morning. The temperature started to plummet, reaching -1°F before day's end. In southern Kentucky, 7 inches of new snow fell. By that point, travel had become virtually impossible. Eastern Air Lines canceled flights for 3 days. Only two of twenty-eight scheduled Greyhound buses arrived in Bowling Green the day after the storm hit. L&N trains were as much as 2 days behind schedule. Hundreds of schools were closed. Tree limbs cracked and fell on power lines already strained by the weight of accumulated ice, bringing them down, and resulting in the loss of electricity throughout the region.

Conditions had changed by February 2, but not necessarily for the better. While the storm had abated, record cold gripped Kentucky and Tennessee. At 4:45 A.M., the temperature in Bowling Green was -20°F, the coldest ever officially recorded to that time.

FIGURE 14. Lexington Herald-Leader *icestorm headlines*
(February 17, 2003).
(Lexington Herald-Leader.)

FIGURE 15. *Effects of the 2003 icestorm in Lexington.*
(*Mark Cornelison/*Lexington Herald-Leader.)

Meanwhile, the storm had left 9 inches of snow and sleet on the
ground in southern Kentucky and 8 inches in central Tennessee.
Crews had by that point already been working for 48 hours
straight trying to restore power and telephone lines. Transportation was still halted. The excessive cold caused unprotected water
pipes to burst. One man even reported that, when he walked outside after standing in front of a heater for a few minutes, the but-
tons on his overcoat shattered instantly. The Western Kentucky
Gas Company reported that it expected record consumption of
gas. Ten days later, the area still had not recovered.

Ultimately, two storm-related deaths were reported in Kentucky,
and estimated damages were $1 million statewide. Estimated
damages across the entire region from Texas to West Virginia affected by the storm were near $100 million. The toll taken on

forested areas, livestock, crops, and fruit trees accounted for over $64 million of that total.

Similar conditions prevailed during the icestorm of January 27, 1971. Freezing rain put a heavy coating of ice over most of the state (only the south-central and eastern portions were unaffected). Then temperatures abruptly dropped below freezing and remained there for several days. Accumulations of up to 3 inches of frozen precipitation were not uncommon, and ice-related accidents caused many injuries. The area hardest hit was that west of Kentucky Lake, where two thousand homes in the Paducah area were reported to have been without electricity. But, across the state, many flowering shrubs and fruit trees suffered serious damage and, consequently, failed to produce spring blooms.

As we have seen, even a hundred years ago icestorms could have a devastating effect on electric service in a major metropolitan area. That effect is even greater today. For example, when an icestorm struck Lexington in February 2003 and a narrow band of freezing rain remained over the city for a number of hours, nearly 1 inch of ice accumulated on trees and power lines, causing widespread damage. Residents described a sound like crackling gunfire as utility poles and limbs snapped, and about half of all businesses and households—an estimated seventy thousand—lost power. Restoring electric service took days, and some residents were without power for up to a week.

Fortunately, icestorms of this magnitude are not common. Until 1951, the only recorded storm of similar magnitude in Kentucky had occurred in February 1899. The Kentucky region can expect a storm producing a 0.75-inch ice load with a concurrent wind gust speed of 30 mph about once every 50 years. Since 1949, fifty icestorms bringing 0.5 inch of ice or more have hit somewhere in the southeastern United States.

FLOODS

The abundant precipitation received during a usual year in Kentucky is not so evenly distributed as the long-term averages indicate. While there is normally ample rainfall in every month, frequently there are dry periods that compensate for periods of excessive rainfall. The irregular topography of the state—especially its numerous valleys—makes it almost certain that local floods will develop whenever heavy rainfall occurs in a relatively short period.

Floods are most frequent in Kentucky during the late winter and early spring months, when the soil is saturated with water and there is less vegetation to retard runoff. A study of the highest flood levels in Kentucky reveals that 63% occurred in the period January–March, 15% in April, 15% in the period May–September, and 7% in the period November–December. No major flooding has occurred in Kentucky during October.

Flooding in Kentucky is of two basic types: localized flash flooding and widespread flooding. The type of flooding experienced is determined by the type of storm affecting a given area.

Flash floods are defined as flood events where the rising water occurs during, or a matter of a few hours after, the associated rainfall. If the damaging water-level increases occur more than a few hours after the rainfall, the event is considered to be a flood, not a flash flood. Narrow valleys are particularly prone to flash flooding because they channel the water quickly downstream. At such times, people who live near the streams receive little or no warning that a flood is imminent. Therefore, flash floods represent a serious threat to life and property. Heavy rainfall is not, however, always a serious threat. If isolated thunderstorms occur over small flatland watersheds containing many larger streams and rivers, they usually cause only a slight increase in water levels a short distance downstream, the runoff being quickly absorbed.

An example of relatively isolated heavy rain occurred on August 2, 1932, over the central Bluegrass region. The precipitation extremes that were recorded reached 6 inches at Richmond and 7.5 inches at Lexington. Lexington received most of its heavy rain from two brief downpours: 3 inches fell from 4:00 to 5:30 A.M., then 2 more inches between 6:00 and 7:00 A.M. Water 4–5 feet deep rushed along Main Street, flooding shops and stores, while residents of low-lying areas had to be evacuated by boat. Six people drowned when their house on Hickman Creek was swept away by the raging water.

Eastern Kentucky, with its narrow valleys and numerous streams, is particularly prone to flash floods—so much so that some streams have been given names like "Troublesome Creek" or "Drowned Branch," suggesting the taxing problems caused when they overflow their banks. One of the worst of eastern Kentucky's flash floods affected Breathitt and Rowan Counties in 1939. During the early morning hours of July 5, 1939, heavy thunderstorms caused a 20-foot wall of water to move down Frozen Creek. Since most of the residents were asleep, they were caught unaware, and over fifty people died. Property damage was estimated at $5 million. Flash flooding was also widespread when heavy rain moved over the region in early April 1977, affecting many counties in the eastern part of the state. Harlan was virtually submerged when the Cumberland River crested 18 feet above flood stage. Flooding caused an estimated $25 million in damage at Pikeville, which saw 6 feet of water in downtown stores. The Red Cross estimated that over a thousand homes were destroyed in Pike County.

Meteorologists have developed methods of analyzing precipitation data and determining the likelihood of these heavy, flash-flood-producing rainfalls occurring. These extreme-precipitation

FIGURE 16. *Flash flood, Floyd County, 2003.*
(Eric Thomas.)

statistics are usually expressed in terms of amount of rain and expected frequency. For example, the greatest amount of rain that Lexington can expect to receive in 6 hours during any given 10-year period is 3.25 inches, and the greatest amount that it can expect to receive in 6 hours during any given 100-year period is 5 inches. The 100-year 6-hour rainfall totals around the state range from about 6 inches in the west to 4.5 inches in the east.

Widespread flooding occurs when heavy rainfall affects a large enough drainage basin that even the larger rivers are affected by the accumulated runoff. As runoff reaches the main water-conveying streams, the magnitude of the potential damage that flooding can cause increases in proportion to the length of the affected rivers and the development that has taken place along them. All of Kentucky is drained by the Ohio and Mississippi Rivers and their tributaries, principal among those being the Big Sandy, Licking, Kentucky, Salt, Green, Tradewater, Cumberland, and Tennessee Rivers. These—and especially the Ohio and the Mississippi—are all long rivers that have seen a great deal of development along their banks, and the potential damage can, thus, be catastrophic.

Heavy rains occurring over even just one or two of the Kentucky river basins can cause regional flooding. For example, the rain that fell on December 7–8, 1978, resulted in 36-hour totals of over 8 inches and produced major flooding of the Kentucky and Licking Rivers. The state capitol building in Frankfort had 3 feet of water in it, and ten thousand people were evacuated from Paintsville when floodwaters rose.

The major flood events that have occurred on the Ohio River are listed in table 1. Note that flood stage is slightly different for each location. *Flood stage* is defined as the level at which overflow of the natural banks of a stream begins to cause damage.

The first well-measured flood after the establishment of standard gauging stations occurred in 1884. February of that year saw above-average precipitation throughout the United States. The greatest excess of rain fell from Tennessee northeast to New England. On February 4, a telegram was sent to Louisville from the U.S. Army's chief signal officer stating that heavy rains were falling in the states of the Ohio Valley. Another telegram was sent later stating that the river was rising at all points and that dangerous floods would occur in the upper Ohio River valley. The heavy rains over the Ohio River valley created major problems all along the river.

In Kentucky, over half of Ashland was submerged as the river left its banks, and only twenty houses remained above water in the town of Catlettsburg in Boyd County. Louisville saw the river rise 1 inch every hour before cresting on February 14 at just a fraction less than 75 feet, 20 feet above flood stage (55 feet). Portions of Louisville remained under water from February 4 to February 25.

ASHLAND		COVINGTON		LOUISVILLE		PADUCAH	
DATE	STAGE (FEET)	DATE	STAGE (FEET)	DATE	STAGE (FEET)	DATE	ST (F
Jan. 27, 1937	74.2	Jan. 26, 1937	80.0	Jan. 27, 1937	85.4	Feb. 2, 1937	6
Apr. 17, 1948	65.9	Feb. 14, 1884	71.1	Mar. 7, 1945	74.4	Apr. 7, 1913	5
Mar. 9, 1945	64.5	Apr. 1, 1913	69.9	Feb. 16, 1884	74.4	Feb. 23, 1884	5
Jan. 2, 1943	64.0	Mar. 7, 1945	69.2	Mar. 13, 1964	73.5	Feb. 13, 1950	5
Mar. 8, 1955	63.8	Feb. 15, 1883	66.3	Apr. 2, 1913	72.7	Mar. 21, 1867	5
Mar. 23, 1936	63.3	Mar. 11, 1964	66.2	Feb. 16, 1883	72.2	Mar. 11, 1997	5
Mar. 21, 1933	62.1	Jan. 21, 1907	65.2	Mar. 7, 1997	70.5	Apr. 3, 1975	5
Feb. 5, 1939	61.2	Apr. 18, 1948	64.8	Feb. 21, 1832	69.9	Mar. 25, 1897	5
Feb. 3, 1950	61.0	Mar. 5, 1997	64.7	Jan. 22, 1907	69.1	Feb. 25, 1883	5
Apr. 23, 1940	61.0	Mar. 21, 1933	63.6	Dec. 17, 1847	68.8	Apr. 17, 1886	5
Flood Stage:	52 feet	Flood Stage:	52 feet	Flood Stage:	55 feet	Flood Stage:	39 f

By February 19, the river at Henderson was above the 42-foot flood stage there. The river gauge, which measured up to 46 feet, 9 inches, was completely submerged, as was Henderson's gasworks. Paducah too suffered extensive flooding, half the town being inundated. Thanks to timely warnings, property owners in Louisville were able to take some precautions. Even so, the total losses sustained by the city were estimated at $100,000.

The most devastating of all the floods to hit Kentucky occurred in January 1937 when the Ohio River set new records along almost its entire length. The extreme flooding of 1937—a singular event to which no other recorded flood on the Ohio has even come close— was caused by a month of extensive heavy precipitation from Kentucky to Pennsylvania. Overall, total precipitation for January was four times its normal amount in the areas surrounding the Ohio River. In fact, there were only eight days in January when the Louisville Weather Office recorded no rain.

The rain began to fall early in the month, and the Ohio River approached flood stage on January 11. Still, forecasters did not expect a major flood—the Maysville crest forecast, for example, was 46 feet, or 4 feet below flood stage. But they had not yet seen the

FIGURE 17. *Front page of* Louisville Courier-Journal *(January 23, 1937)*.

(Louisville Courier-Journal.)

FIGURE 18. *Widespread inundation of Louisville
during the January 1937 flood.*
(Louisville Courier-Journal.)

most significant rainfall, which began on January 13 and continued through January 24, the very worst rains coming on January
22 and 23 and bringing, for example, 5.82 inches to Louisville.
These heavy rains, coupled with an already swollen river, caused a
rapid rise in water level. On January 22, the Ohio at Carrollton
was observed to rise a full 7 feet in 7 hours. Flood stage at Maysville was finally exceeded by 25 feet. The river at Louisville rose 6.3
feet between January 21 and January 22. The entire Ohio was
above flood stage by January 24.

FIGURE 19. *A Louisville neighborhood flooded in 1937.*
Note the ice that formed during the prolonged cold.
(Photographic Archives, Special Collections,
University of Louisville.)

At Louisville, the river ultimately reached 85.4 feet, or 30 feet above flood stage, when it crested on January 27. This is the only time it has been known to reach a height above 80 feet since the first readings were taken in 1832. Water levels stayed above flood stage for 25 consecutive days, keeping cities along the river under water. The previous flood record set in 1884 had been broken by 11 feet. In Paducah, the river crested at 60.6 feet on February 2, and the entire city was forced to evacuate. Damage throughout the Ohio Valley was extensive.

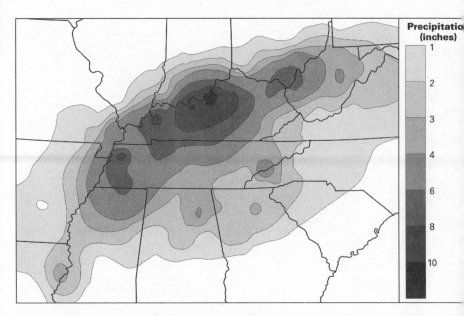

FIGURE 20. *Total precipitation (inches), February 28–March 3, 1997.*
(Data provided by Kentucky Climate Center.)

Along the Ohio River the city hardest hit was Louisville. Municipal power and water services failed, 70% of the city was under water, and 175,000 people were forced to leave their homes. The human impact was compounded by the power failure. Even those able to remain in their homes had no heat. The major newspaper in Louisville, the *Courier-Journal,* could not operate its printing presses. The staff resorted to assembling single-page editions for January 25 and 26 and printing them in Shelbyville, and, from January 27 through February 5, the paper was printed on the presses of the *Lexington Herald-Leader.* Printing resumed in Louisville only on February 6, municipal power having finally been restored after 13 days of darkness.

The high water was not, of course, limited to the Ohio River. Every stream in the state had swollen beyond its banks. The rising water of the Kentucky River flooded Frankfort, and inmates in the penitentiary located in the capital city at the time rioted, believing

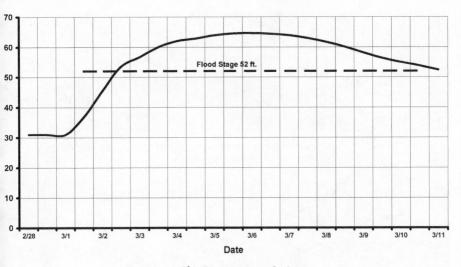

FIGURE 21. *Ohio River stages at Covington
(Cincinnati gauge) during the 1997 flood.
(National Weather Service Ohio River Forecast Center.)*

that the rising water would trap them in their cells. Finally, the warden agreed to disperse the convicts under armed guard to nearby counties, where they were held in local jails until the flood threat abated.

Fifty thousand families across Kentucky were driven from their homes and kept from them for an extended period because of the persistence of the flooding. The Weather Bureau reported that, statewide, total flood damage was $250 million, an incredible sum in 1937.

Most recently, heavy regional rainfall caused extreme flooding in parts of Kentucky in 1997. On March 1, a severe-weather situation developed when thunderstorms with tornadoes and very heavy rainfall formed along a nearly stationary front extending from Texas to West Virginia. Unusually heavy rainfall (figure 20) fell from northeast Arkansas through western Tennessee and into much of Kentucky, southern Indiana, Ohio, and West Virginia— on ground in many places already almost completely saturated

FIGURE 22. *Downtown Falmouth, inundated during the 1997 flood.*
(Kentucky National Guard.)

from the unusually heavy precipitation (both snow and rain) of the past few months. In parts of north-central Kentucky, rainfall rates averaged almost 1 inch per hour for a 12-hour period.

The heavy rainfall caused the Ohio River to rise and crest in Louisville on March 7 at about 16 feet above flood stage—an example of how rapidly a large river like the Ohio can rise when heavy rain falls throughout the river basin. Figure 21 shows the stages observed over a 12-day period at Covington, where the river rose rapidly from a reading of about 30 feet on the gauge on March 1 to over 60 feet by March 4.

The northern Kentucky town of Falmouth, where floodwaters reached depths of over 8 feet, was almost completely destroyed. In Louisville, the storm generated a total of 13.04 inches of rain over the period between February 28 and March 3, with 10.48 inches falling in one 24-hour period, setting a new state record. What made this new record particularly surprising was the fact that, according to long-term rainfall statistics at least, even a rainfall total of 7 inches in 24 hours can be expected in Louisville only once in 100 years.

By the time the storm was over, flooding had killed twenty-one people in Kentucky and damaged or destroyed over seventy-five thousand homes. More than a hundred Kentucky counties were declared federal disaster areas. Over the entire multistate area affected by the storm, sixty-seven people died, and there was over $1 billion in damages.

SEVERE STORMS

The extremely temperate weather conditions that Kentucky enjoys much of the time are, as we have seen, not without occasional excesses. Fortunately, the state is far enough from a coastline that it does not experience the devastating winds of hurricanes, but severe thunderstorms and tornadoes do occasionally threaten human life and cause extensive damage. These storms, which can occur in any month, can be accompanied by strong damaging winds, severe lightning, and hail.

In 2002, Kentucky led the nation in insured losses, with nearly $1 billion in damage caused by catastrophic natural disasters, a *catastrophic natural disaster* being any event that causes more than $25 million in damage and affects a significant number of insurers and policyholders. The losses stemmed from such events as floods, thunderstorms, hail, and tornadoes.

THUNDERSTORMS

Thunderstorms affect relatively small areas but are among the most dangerous of weather events. They form in the presence of adequate moisture and a rapidly rising air mass, the latter condition being the result of either an unstable air mass rising on its own as it warms, most commonly on a hot summer day, or any air mass being forced upward by an approaching cold front. Thunderstorms can occur as isolated single storms 5–10 miles in diameter or as clusters of storms organized as a squall line, a narrow band sometimes over 100 miles long oriented parallel to a cold front and 50–100 miles in advance of it.

In Kentucky, during the warm months of about April–September, afternoon thunderstorms most frequently develop over the western portions of the state and then move east. The terrain is more conducive to thunderstorm development in western Kentucky than in eastern because the land is flatter, allowing more intense heating of the ground and lifting of the air. The lifetime of a thunderstorm can be less than an hour, but sometimes large cells grow into what are known to meteorologists as *supercells*. There is no specific meteorological definition of a supercell, but it is generally considered to be a rotating thunderstorm that has a well-defined circulation. It grows to a greater height than most and persists for several hours. A supercell can remain nearly stationary, or it can move a great distance, depending on the strength of steering winds aloft. Storms considered to be supercells are often associated with tornadoes, damaging winds, and large hail.

Several factors account for the dangerous nature of thunderstorms. Chief among them is the flash flooding that, as we have seen, thunderstorms can bring. Flash flooding is the number one cause of death associated with thunderstorms, resulting as it does in more than 140 fatalities nationwide every year. Close behind flash flooding is lightning. All thunderstorms generate lightning, which, when it reaches the ground, can damage utility lines, set fire to structures, and even kill people. On average, eighty deaths and three hundred injuries are attributed to lightning each year in the United States.

Also dangerous are the strong, sudden increases in wind speed that can be associated with thunderstorms. The downdrafts of cold, heavy air within a thunderstorm reach the ground and spread out, sometimes causing very strong gusts. A particularly dangerous type of wind, called a *downburst*, is a small area of rapidly descending air beneath a thunderstorm. Downbursts can cause damage equivalent to that caused by a tornado, although these winds move in a straight line. Downbursts have been known

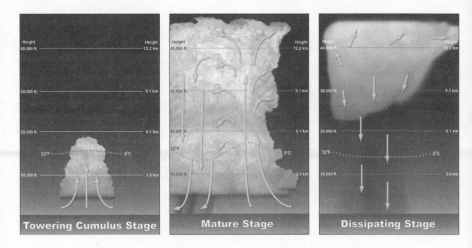

FIGURE 23. *Life cycle of a thunderstorm.*
(National Weather Service.)

to shatter windows, uproot trees, damage roofs, and even over-
turn mobile homes. At several airport weather-observing stations
in Kentucky, wind gusts over 80 mph have been recorded with this
type of phenomenon, and, in a thunderstorm at Owensboro, a
peak wind of 92 mph was once observed.

The National Weather Service considers any thunderstorm to
be severe if it produces winds of 58 mph or stronger, hail at least
0.75 inch in diameter, or a tornado.

HAIL

Severe thunderstorms occasionally produce hail, and, although
hailstones can be large, they are usually less than 0.5 inch in diameter. Hail is not common in Kentucky. Even so, significant hail
events occur in all regions of the state. Usually, a major hail event
will cover several counties, but hailstorms have been known to
affect small areas—for example, the isolated storm that struck
Lexington on May 21, 1917, with hailstones 3.25 inches in diameter. Damaging hail has been observed in Kentucky during all
months but is most common during the spring and early summer.

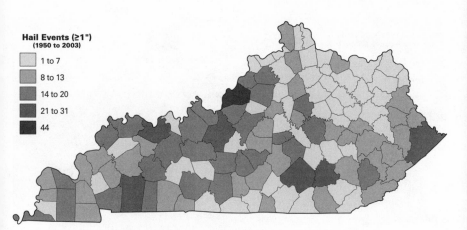

Hail Events (≥1")
(1950 to 2003)

- 1 to 7
- 8 to 13
- 14 to 20
- 21 to 31
- 44

FIGURE 24. *Number of hail events where the hail was
larger than 1 inch in diameter, 1950-2003.
(Data provided by National Climatic Data Center.)*

A tabulation of hailstorms in the state indicates that over 80% occurred between the hours of 1:00 P.M. and 7:00 P.M. and that almost all occurred between noon and 9:00 P.M.

Hail forms in well-developed thunderstorms where there is
strong upward convection, or the upward movement of air.
These thunderstorms can be of two types: those occurring in
clusters along or slightly ahead of rapidly moving cold fronts
(squall lines) and those that develop in isolation. Hailstones are
created when strong upward currents within a thunderstorm
carry raindrops high enough that they freeze to form small hailstones, which gravity then pulls down into the lower, warmer
zone, where they collect a layer of water. Hailstones often get
caught in another strong updraft and again carried high enough
for the layer of water to freeze. In strong thunderstorms, this process can be repeated several times, adding many layers of ice to
the stone before it finally becomes heavy enough to fall to earth.
During this time, the thunderstorm is usually at its maximum development in terms of height and also producing very heavy rainfall with strong, gusty winds.

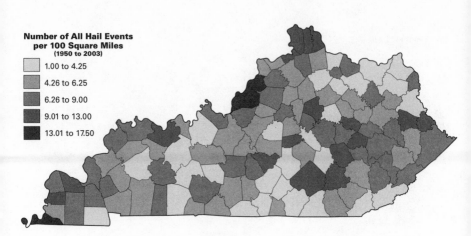

FIGURE 25. *Number of hail events per 100 square miles, 1950–2003.*
(Data provided by National Climatic Data Center.)

The National Weather Service determines hail size on the basis of a standard scale in which the diameter of hail is described in terms of common household objects (see table 2). This is a generalized scale because hailstones, especially very large ones, will have irregular shapes, rather than being perfect spheres.

In comparison with that in some other states, the hail risk in Kentucky is not particularly high. The number of days with a hailstorm at any particular location averages only 2–3 during a typical year. The distribution of hail across the state does not show any particular pattern. A study of insurance losses in Kentucky indicates that property damage due to hail accounts for only about 0.005% of residential property damage each year—one-tenth the figure for northwestern Kansas, the portion of the United States that sees the most property damage from hailstorms.

Interestingly, despite the low residential-property-damage figures, Kentucky ranks high nationally in terms of annual crop loss from hailstorms. This is probably because one of Kentucky's major cash crops is tobacco, which has a high value per acre. If a hailstorm does not completely kill a field of tobacco plants, the damage that it causes to the leaves can seriously reduce the

TABLE 2. HAIL-SIZE DESCRIPTIONS USED BY THE NATIONAL WEATHER SERVICE

Hail Diameter	Description
0.25 inch	Pea size
0.5 inch	Small marble size
0.75 inch (severe threshold)	Dime/penny/large marble size
0.875 inch	Nickel size
1 inch	Quarter size
1.25 inches	Half dollar size
1.5 inches	Walnut or Ping Pong ball size
1.75 inches	Golf ball size
2 inches	Hen egg size
2.5 inches	Tennis ball size
2.75 inches	Baseball size
3 inches	Teacup size
4 inches	Grapefruit size
4.5 inches	Softball size

crop's value to the grower. Thus, even if a hailstorm affects only one or two counties, the potential exists for it to cause significant monetary loss.

Although hailstorms may not be as frequent in Kentucky as they are elsewhere, they have caused frightening experiences for many of the state's residents. One of the most damaging hailstorms in Kentucky history was on August 1, 1952, in Boyle County, where losses totaled $810,000. Crops, chiefly tobacco, were destroyed or damaged over an area of about 11 square miles.

Residents of south-central Kentucky will long remember the hailstorm that occurred on April 16, 1998. Stormy weather developed ahead of an approaching cold front, and, by midafternoon, a large supercell thunderstorm formed in northern Logan County and then moved into Warren County, where it brought high winds and dropped hail along a path through Bowling Green and surrounding communities. The storm then pushed into Barren County and later hit Metcalfe County, its high winds and the tornadoes that it spawned causing extensive damage. There were two fatalities reported at Glasgow in Barren County that day as one of the tornadoes swept through causing $10 million in damage.

FIGURE 26. *Hailstones that fell in Bowling Green, April 16, 1998.*
(*Joe Imel*/Bowling Green Daily News.)

Hailstones the size of baseballs smashed the windshields of cars and trucks, broke storefront windows, and pounded the roofs and siding of homes, schools, and businesses. In Warren County alone, hail, wind, and rain damaged more than eleven thousand homes and an estimated ten thousand automobiles and damaged or destroyed sixteen airplanes. Other reported damage included $10 million worth to the roof and air-conditioning system at the Greenwood Mall and enough to the roof of the Bowling Green high school to cause extensive water damage and force the building to be closed for the duration of the school year. No hail-related fatalities were reported, but many people injured by hail and flying glass were treated at local hospitals.

The combination of straight-line winds, tornadoes, and large hail resulted in estimated storm costs in excess of $500 million, the highest hail-related loss in state history. Cleanup and repair of the widespread damage continued for months. With local contractors overwhelmed, contractors from neighboring cities and states set

FIGURE 27. *Hail damage in Bowling Green, April 16, 1998.*
(*Wales Hunter*/Bowling Green Daily News.)

up temporary offices, and many hired migrant construction work-
ers to complete the work.

The next greatest hail loss, amounting to $400,000, was on May
17, 1953, in Henderson County, which saw heavy damage to crops.
In Corydon, Kentucky, practically every building was damaged.
Even furniture in homes and the merchandise in stores suffered
damage when hailstones crashed through windows, permitting
rain to deluge the interiors.

Uniontown, in Union County, experienced a $200,000 loss on
the same day. Almost all residences and nine businesses were
damaged. Hail knocked holes in many roofs, allowing rain to flood
the interiors. After the storm, automobiles were described as
looking as if they had "been beaten by hammers."

A 30-minute hailstorm on September 13, 1946, over a path 5
miles wide in Franklin, Owen, and Henry Counties resulted in a
loss of $200,000, mostly to the tobacco crop. In some places, the
ground was covered to a depth of 5 inches by small hailstones that
remained frozen solid for several hours.

An outbreak of thunderstorms that occurred on May 1, 2002, was notable for the long swath of hail damage caused across the state. The first report of large hail came from near Brandenburg, in Meade County, about 5:00 P.M., when 2-inch hailstones fell. The storms moved east across Louisville and central Kentucky, with hailstone reports reaching up to 4.5 inches from the area around Bardstown to Lebanon. About 9:00 P.M. they finally reached Harlan, where the last reported hail was golf ball sized and caused about $30,000 in damage, mostly to vehicles. Total estimated storm damage statewide was about $500 million.

The disastrous thunderstorms that struck much of central Kentucky late on April 3, 1974, are recalled mostly for the tornadoes that accompanied them, but they were also preceded by very damaging hailstorms in western Kentucky earlier in the afternoon. About 1:30 P.M. that day, a hailstorm struck Sturgis in Union County and lasted 20 minutes. Hailstones 2.5 inches in diameter caused extensive damage, and the heavy rains that followed were responsible for minor flooding. At 2:00 P.M., hailstones as large as baseballs pounded Princeton in Caldwell County, causing extensive damage to automobiles, roofs, and windows. Some hailstones measured nearly 5 inches across and weighed nearly half a pound.

The record hail accumulation in Kentucky occurred on November 22, 1967, when hail up to 0.5 inch in diameter accumulated on the ground near Summer Shade in Metcalfe County—up to 6 inches deep in some spots. This example of accumulation is, of course, extreme, as are the examples of record size given above. While averages vary county by county across the state, accumulation is usually minimal, and large hail events (those producing hail with a diameter of 0.75 inch or greater) are rare.

TORNADOES

A tornado is a violently rotating funnel-shaped cloud that descends from the base of a thunderstorm and touches the ground. In some ways it is similar to a mini low-pressure system with very low pressure in the center and winds rotating counterclockwise around the perimeter. One of the challenges to modern weather

FIGURE 28. *A tornado on the ground.*
(National Oceanic and Atmospheric Administration/
Department of Commerce.)

forecasting is determining whether a thunderstorm will be mild, with a little lightning and thunder, or become a storm that produces a tornado with weather so severe that people are killed or seriously injured. The factors to be taken into consideration include the instability of the air, vertical wind shear, the amount of available moisture, and the lifting motions of the atmosphere, all of which can vary considerably from day to day.

It would be a great oversimplification to assume that tornadoes form any time cold Canadian air moves over Kentucky and meets

FIGURE 29. *A funnel cloud aloft.*
(National Oceanic and Atmospheric Administration/
Department of Commerce.)

warm, moist air from the Gulf of Mexico. Many thunderstorms form under these conditions but never even come close to producing a tornado. Even when the large-scale environment is extremely favorable for tornadic thunderstorms, not every thunderstorm spawns a tornado. Scientists still do not completely understand why this is the case. The most deadly and destructive tornadoes usually result from the supercell thunderstorms that have a rotating circulation. Still, some supercells can produce vivid lightning, damaging hail, and gusty winds, but no tornadoes.

Scientists studied tornadoes for many years before they were ever able to actually measure the wind speeds in one. Initially, speeds could only be estimated on the basis of the damage that was observed. However, technological developments using Doppler radar can now register the speed of winds in a tornado by measuring the velocity with which the raindrops and other particles move. On May 3, 1999, research meteorologists set up a mobile Doppler weather-radar unit near Oklahoma City and observed a record wind speed of 318 mph in a tornado that hit the suburbs of that city. This is the fastest wind ever recorded, and that particular tornado killed four people and destroyed about 250 homes with its devastating fury.

It is not just the force of its winds that makes a tornado so destructive, however, but also the very low pressure at its center. As a tornado passes over a building, the air pressure outside drops suddenly, and, when the air inside the building cannot escape fast enough to equalize the pressure on the interior walls and the roof, the structure collapses outward.

Whenever a supercell thunderstorm develops a tornado, the funnel-shaped appendage will sometimes skip along the ground and sometimes hang in the air like a rope. The path cut by a tornado on the ground can range in width from a hundred yards to half a mile—the wider tornadoes leaving lesser damage as far as 500 yards on either side of the path itself—and it can range in length from a few hundred feet to a hundred miles. Tornadoes move along their forward paths at speeds ranging from 35 to 65 mph.

Since tornadoes are spawned by thunderstorms, they are most likely to occur during the afternoon, when thunderstorm development is greatest, and then persist into the evening hours. If the day is divided into four 6-hour periods, we find that about 50% of tornadoes in Kentucky occur between noon and 6:00 P.M., 25% between 6:00 P.M. and midnight, 12.5% between midnight and 6:00 A.M., and 12.5% between 6:00 A.M. and noon.

Between 1950 and 2003, tornadoes are known to have been responsible for 115 deaths and over twenty-five hundred injuries in the state. According to the National Weather Service, an average year in the United States sees about twelve hundred tornadoes and seventy tornado-related deaths.

Kentucky is unlike those states—many located west of the Mississippi River—where tornadoes are a routine occurrence each year, especially in the spring. Between 1950 and 2003, a total of 635 tornadoes were reported in Kentucky, for an average of about a dozen per year. During that period, only the year 1953 passed without a tornado being reported. The annual number observed ranges from none to the 1997 record of thirty-nine. The single-day record—set during the record tornado outbreak across the Midwest on April 3, 1974—is twenty-seven.

The month that normally has the greatest amount of tornado activity in Kentucky is April, when clashes between warm and cold air masses are still likely. About 29% of all tornadoes in Kentucky occur in April. However, tornadoes have been reported in the state in every month. Even January, the coldest month of the year, has tornadoes; one in January 1959, for example, was responsible for three deaths. The fewest tornadoes are reported in October, the driest month.

Reliable tornado statistics date back only to about 1950. During the nineteenth century and the early part of the twentieth, tornadoes occurring in sparsely populated areas likely went unnoticed or were reported only to a local newspaper. Since 1950, improved communications and a greater awareness of the need to report tornadoes mean that most tornadoes are now accounted for.

The violent wind and rapidly changing pressure associated with tornadoes often cause odd and almost unbelievable types of damage. Even some documented accounts are hard to believe. For example, a 1919 tornado in Minnesota split open a tree, jammed an automobile in the crack, and then clamped the tree shut again. Tornadoes often carry objects long distances. One 1877 Illinois tornado carried the spire, vane, and gilded ball from a Methodist church 15 miles. One in South Dakota in 1923 tore a 6-inch-wide,

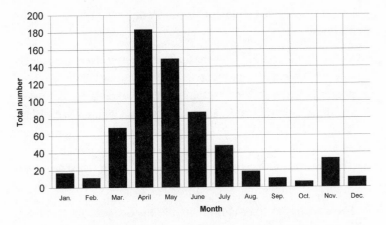

FIGURE 30. *Number of Kentucky tornadoes observed by month, 1950-2003.*
(Data provided by National Climatic Data Center.)

13-foot-long steel I beam from a highway bridge and carried it an eighth of a mile before driving it through a cottonwood tree 15 inches in diameter without splitting or toppling it. There have even been reports of herds of cattle carried aloft by tornadoes, looking like gigantic birds in the sky. During the 1974 outbreak in Kentucky, a large number of livestock were killed by tornadoes that caught them grazing in open fields.

A review of accounts indicates that tornadoes can occur in almost any section of the state and in any terrain, hilltop or valley bottom. In general, the greatest number occur in the western and northern sections, the fewest in the eastern. About 80% of all Kentucky tornadoes approach from the west–southwest. And, during the average year, tornadoes are reported at widely scattered locations across the state.

It is an interesting coincidence that the first white man to record his explorations in Kentucky encountered a tornado-like storm. Dr. Thomas Walker led a party from Virginia into Kentucky in 1750. They came through the Cumberland Gap, explored that eastern section of Kentucky, and then crossed the Big Sandy River to return home across what is now central West Virginia. When the party was in the vicinity of Salyersville or Paintsville on

June 4, they survived a violent storm. Walker recorded the event in his diary:

> Got to Falling creek and went up it till 5 in the afternoon, when a very black cloud appearing, we turn'd out our horses, got tent poles up, and were just stretching a tent, when it began to rain and hail, and was succeeded by a violent wind which blew down our tent and a great many trees around it, several large ones within 30 yards of the tent. We all left the place in confusion and ran different ways for shelter. After the storm was over, we met at the tent, and found all safe.

The next day Walker commented in his diary: "This morning we went up the creek about 3 miles, and then were obliged to leave it, the timber being so blown down that we could not get through." The problems caused by the storm plagued the party even a week later when they were near the Big Sandy River. On June 10, Walker wrote: "Being in very bad ground for our horses, we concluded to move. We were very much hindered by the trees that had blown down on Monday last."

Several years later, reference was made to another tornado in Kentucky. In the late winter of 1778–79, George Rogers Clark led a party to Vincennes to assault the English outpost where the British were encouraging the Indians to attack frontier settlements. They captured Lord Henry Hamilton, known as the "hair buyer" because of the bounty that he had placed on white men's scalps. Hamilton kept a meticulous diary while he was being transported via an oak boat down the Wabash River and up the Ohio to Louisville. On March 27, when he and his captors were about 2 days below Louisville, near the present site of Brandenburg, Hamilton noted:

> I landed with Major Hay and Mr. Bellefeuille on the east side of the river to get a view of the ravages occasioned by a whirlwind or hurricane—we had some difficulty in scrambling to the top of the cliff, great craggs and large trees tumbled together in confusion obliging us sometimes to creep and sometimes to climb—when we got to the top we saw the progress of this vein

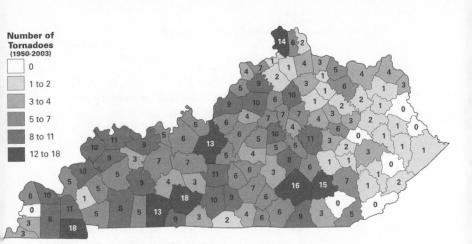

FIGURE 31. *Number of tornadoes reported by county, 1950–2003.*
(Data provided by National Climatic Data Center.)

of wind which was in a straight line across the River, and thro the wood which was mowed downed at about 20 or 25 feet from the ground, the vista opened being as regular as if laid down by a line.

One hundred ninety-five years later, almost to the day, a tornado touched down on April 3, 1974, in Breckinridge County, very near the same location, and killed thirty-one people at Brandenburg before crossing the Ohio River into Indiana.

The 53-year period 1950–2003 in Kentucky saw an average of 17.3 tornadoes per 10,000 square miles per year. When the data are broken down by county, it turns out that no tornadoes were observed in seven of Kentucky's 120 counties—Carlisle, Harlan, Knott, Knox, Lawrence, Martin, and Wolfe.

The intensity of a tornado in terms of wind speed and probable damage is ranked on a scale of 0–5 (from lowest to highest intensity): the Fujita Scale (or F Scale), developed by Dr. T. Theodore Fujita of the University of Chicago. The Fujita Scale is outlined in table 3. From 1950 to 2003 in Kentucky, there were 119 F0 tornadoes, 236 F1 tornadoes, 158 F2 tornadoes, 82 F3 tornadoes,

TABLE 3. FUJITA SCALE FOR RANKING TORNADO INTENSITY

SCALE	WIND ESTIMATE (MPH)	TYPICAL DAMAGE
F0	‹ 73	*Light damage.* Some damage to chimneys; branches broken off trees; shallow-rooted trees pushed over; signboards damaged
F1	73–112	*Moderate damage.* Surface peeled off roofs; mobile homes pushed off foundations or overturned; moving cars blown off roads
F2	113–157	*Considerable damage.* Roofs torn off frame houses; mobile homes demolished; boxcars overturned; large trees snapped or uprooted; light-object missiles generated; cars lifted off ground
F3	158–206	*Severe damage.* Roofs and some walls torn off well-constructed houses; trains overturned; most trees in forest uprooted; heavy cars lifted off ground and thrown
F4	207–60	*Devastating damage.* Well-constructed houses leveled; structures with weak foundations blown away some distance; cars thrown and large missiles generated
F5	261–318	*Incredible damage.* Strong frame houses leveled off foundations and swept away; car-sized missiles fly through the air in excess of 100 meters (109 yards); trees debarked; incredible phenomena occur

37 F4 tornadoes, and 3 F5 tornadoes. All the F5 tornado occurrences were on April 4, 1974.

There has been some controversy over whether two of the F5 tornadoes were actually the same tornado. Breckinridge County was struck first, then, shortly afterward, adjacent Meade County. The similar intensities of the two storms and the alignment of their paths suggest to some one tornado, not two. If that was, in fact, the case, the state's total of F5 tornadoes would be two, not three. However, the official records of the National Climatic Data Center list the Breckinridge County and the Meade County tornadoes separately, for a total of three F5 tornadoes.

The April 3–4, 1974, tornado outbreak marks one of the worst in U.S. history, with a total of 148 tornadoes reported nationwide. The weather map on the morning of April 3 showed a low-pressure center in Kansas with a cold front extending south into Texas.

FIGURE 32. *Tornado damage in Brandenburg, April 3, 1974.*
(Louisville Courier-Journal.)

Ahead of the low-pressure center, a strong flow of southerly winds from the Gulf of Mexico was bringing warm and moist air into the Ohio Valley. This was the perfect setup for the development of severe weather, and, by afternoon, at least three separate squall lines of very intense thunderstorms had developed. The first indication that a super outbreak of tornadoes would occur was when a series of eleven twisters struck central Illinois in the early afternoon.

The first of the tornadoes to strike Kentucky touched down around 3:25 P.M. that day in Boone County. It was an F5 tornado and caused incredible damage. Fortunately, there were no fatalities, but twenty people were injured. The next tornado touched down about 5 miles southwest of Hardinsburg at 3:40 P.M. It remained on the ground and continued across Breckinridge County into Meade

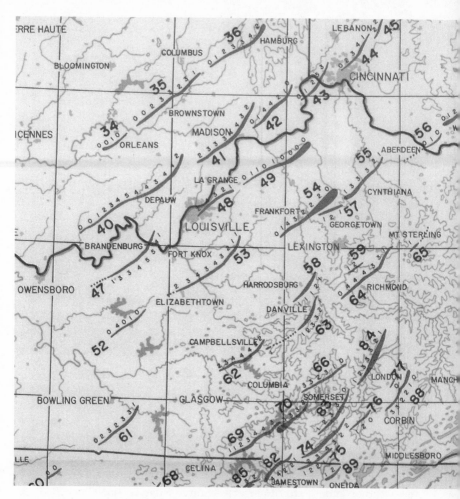

FIGURE 33. *Individual tornado paths in Kentucky on April 3, 1974.*
The larger number next to each track represents its chronological sequence
among the total of 148 storms reported during the course of the
multistate outbreak. The smaller numbers along the tracks
represent the intensity at that point.
(Texas Tech University Wind Science and
Engineering Research Center Archives.)

FIGURE 34. *Bonded whiskey warehouses struck by a tornado.*
(Louisville Courier-Journal.)

County, growing in intensity as it traveled. The twister struck Brandenburg around 4:10 P.M., then crossed the Ohio River into Harrison County, Indiana. The Brandenburg tornado, another F5, is the most destructive tornado ever recorded in Kentucky. It devastated the business district of Brandenburg, killing 31, injuring 257, and destroying or severely damaging three to four hundred homes.

The tornadoes continued through the evening, with a total of twenty-seven finally identified that first day. Many of these struck after dark, when visual detection is almost impossible. The last one occurred between 11:30 P.M. and midnight, moving across Pulaski and Rockcastle Counties. In figure 33 we see a poststorm map showing the paths of the tornadoes that moved across Kentucky and neighboring Indiana and Ohio. The tornadoes that touched down in Kentucky on April 3 left behind 77 dead, 1,377 injured, and over $110 million in damages. A total of thirty-nine Kentucky counties reported tornado damage from this outbreak. Kentucky and nine other states were declared disaster areas.

Certainly, the 1974 outbreak will remain fixed in the minds of those who lived through it, but there were earlier outbreaks in the state that were nearly as serious. For example, although much smaller in scale overall, the outbreak the night of March 27, 1890—when at least five tornadoes struck the state—left more people dead: seventy-six in Louisville alone, thirty more in the surrounding area, and anywhere from twenty to sixty in other parts of the state. In terms of cleanup costs, however, it is hard to say which outbreak was more expensive, given the degree to which inflation has increased replacement costs. Still, when the costs in Louisville alone are considered, the estimated $2.5 million in damage incurred in 1890, compared to the over $5 million in damage in 1974, makes it likely that the storms hitting the city on those occasions were of roughly similar magnitudes.

9

DROUGHT

A drought is considered by meteorologists to be a period of abnormally dry weather of sufficient length within a region to cause a serious imbalance between precipitation and water needs, thus resulting in crop damage or water supply shortages. Drought conditions can build from one month to another and will end only when rainfall has been adequate to restore soil moisture and stream flows to the levels usual for the time of year in question. In some cases, drought will persist for several years before conditions return to normal. Because different regions have different climates, however, drought conditions are determined region by region. What would be considered drought-producing rainfall in Kentucky would be considered overly abundant rainfall in Arizona.

The degree to which actual rainfall lags behind required rainfall can be used to categorize a drought as *mild, moderate, severe,* or *extreme.* Each category represents a progressively more serious effect on farming, industry, and municipal water supplies. In Kentucky, mild droughts are not uncommon even in years that, overall, receive adequate rainfall. In such cases, several consecutive months of below-normal rainfall result in a slight degree of soil-moisture deficiency and some reduction in crop yields. During extreme drought, crops fail completely, groundwater supplies disappear, and entire stands of large trees die.

One of the methods most commonly employed by meteorologists to evaluate drought is the Palmer Drought Severity Index (PDSI), developed in the 1960s by W. C. Palmer, a meteorologist

TABLE 4. PALMER DROUGHT SEVERITY INDEX CLASSIFICATIONS

INDEX	DESCRIPTION
4.0 or more	Extremely wet
3.0 to 3.99	Very wet
2.0 to 2.99	Moderately wet
1.0 to 1.99	Slightly wet
0.5 to 0.99	Incipient wet spell
0.49 to −0.49	Near normal
−0.5 to −0.99	Incipient dry spell
−1.9 to −1.99	Mild drought
−2.0 to −2.99	Moderate drought
−3.0 to −3.99	Severe drought
−4.0 or less	Extreme drought

in the government weather service. The PDSI takes into consideration both rainfall and estimated evaporation in order to provide standardized measurements of moisture conditions that can be compared across locations and months. It is most effective when used to measure impacts to industries, such as agriculture, that are particularly sensitive to soil-moisture conditions. But it is also useful as a real-time drought-monitoring tool and has been used to trigger a region's drought contingency plans. PDSI categories and their descriptions are given in table 4.

Weather data from January 1895 to December 2003 have been used to calculate the PDSI month by month over a period of more than 100 years for the four climatic districts in Kentucky. The results—shown in the appendix—illustrate the frequency and severity of drought in each of the four areas.

Studies of drought throughout the United States have revealed that the dry weather experienced in the early 1930s and the mid-1950s affected not only Kentucky but also much of the central part of the nation. Looking even further back, we learn that the central United States experienced serious drought during the periods 1911-17, 1887-93, and 1865-70. The records show a tendency for drought to become widespread and serious at intervals of about 20-25 years. Some meteorologists believe the cause to be a predominance of high pressure over the central portions of the

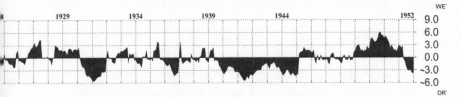

FIGURE 35. *Palmer Drought Severity Index for western Kentucky, 1924-52.*
Index values less than -3 indicate severe drought conditions. Note the extended
drought periods 1930-32 and 1940-45.
(Data provided by National Climatic Data Center.)

country that is somehow connected with sunspot activity. No
satisfactory explanation of how sunspot activity could affect
weather systems has yet been put forward, however, so this theory
remains just that—a theory.

The most serious drought ever recorded in Kentucky occurred
during 1930, when annual rainfall totals averaged only 25-30
inches. During the growing season (April–October), only 51% of
the normal rainfall occurred. As conditions became increasingly
dry, waves of heat in July added to the discomfort by breaking
temperature records and causing enormous crop damage. By July,
pastures had been practically destroyed, compelling farmers to
feed their limited supply of hay to, or sell, their livestock. By August and September, large creeks had run dry, and, by fall, wells
and springs never known to fail were dry as well. Springs were
still failing in December. As a result of crop failure, loss of stock,
and enforced idleness, a considerable number of tenant farmers
and farmworkers were reduced to a state of destitution.

That year the Ohio River between Covington and Cincinnati
dropped to just 3 feet deep. Health officials issued a warning for
people not to swim in the river because its stagnant condition
had caused typhoid germs to develop. Ultimately, 86 of Kentucky's 120 counties were placed on a national disaster relief list.
A letter written to the *Kentucky Post* on August 8, 1930, jokingly attributed the drought to God's anger at the radical prohibitionists,
who had advocated against the sale of alcohol. This is a seemingly

late response, the Prohibition Act having been passed in 1920, 10 years earlier.

Although not nearly as severe as the drought of 1930, a summer dry spell in 1913 caused Kentucky farmers considerable losses. This was because, even though annual precipitation levels were near normal in 1913, very dry weather from April to September resulted in a disastrous crop season. The moisture deficit continued into 1914, when many locations, especially in western Kentucky, experienced annual precipitation that was almost 10 inches below normal.

There are references to droughts in several years during the late 1830s and mid-1840s that must have caused some hardships, but no official rainfall records are available to document them. The dryness of 1839 must certainly have impressed the editor of the *Kentucky Gazette* because he wrote the following in the September 5 issue: "We have not had one old fashion good rain for upwards of a year. The perpetual complaints of the drought have caused, we apprehend, fears on the part of our farmers, of the great scarcity of provisions, judging from the excessive prices of some articles on the market. One dollar and fifteen cents per bushel was asked for corn meal in our market of yesterday! It is a mistake— there is no danger of starvation."

The first well-documented drought that occurred in Kentucky after routine weather observations were established came in 1897. By the end of the summer, most of the streams ran dry, and the supply of water in many springs ran out. Marshals guarded town wells to ensure the equitable distribution of water. A brief but intense drought was to develop in 1908, creating widespread hardship. Rainfall totals for that year were as low as the 28.15 inches recorded at Williamstown.

In more recent times, extreme dryness developed over western Kentucky during the summer of 1952. Low rainfall amounts continued into 1953, for which year Carrollton recorded only 24.10 inches. In Louisville, a record was set for the most consecutive dry days: 36 (September 20–October 25) without measurable rainfall.

Serious drought also developed over much of the Midwest and the Ohio and Tennessee Valleys in 1988. Kentucky was particularly hard hit because the 1988 drought actually represented an intensification of a drought that in many areas of the state had begun in 1987. The PDSI values in most districts dropped to -3 and even -4, indicative of severe drought, and several communities in Kentucky had to resort to restrictions on water use.

Beginning in May 1988, a series of broad ridges of high pressure began moving across the central United States in what is called a *wave train*. This pattern persisted through the middle of June and set up the chain of events that contributed to that summer's drought. First, the polar jet stream shifted farther north than normal. That shift caused all the low-pressure systems that normally produce rain to move north into Canada. The flow of winds from the Gulf of Mexico, an important moisture source for summer convection in Kentucky, was weak as a result of the prevailing circulation pattern.

Rainfall across the Midwest and Great Plains averaged around 50% of normal for the months of May, June, and July. This lack of summer rain, combined with the effects of a drier-than-normal spring, contributed to very low stream flow and river levels. Barge traffic on the Mississippi River was affected for several months in the fall and winter. The river was even closed to navigation south of Saint Louis in December, costing millions of dollars in lost revenues.

Agricultural losses were high as nonirrigated crops withered on the stalk when temperatures soared. Commodity prices rose to unprecedented levels. Corn prices climbed as high as $3.50 per bushel, $1.40 over the seasonal average of $2.10 per bushel. Soybeans reached $10.00 per bushel in mid-June before falling to around $8.00 per bushel by the end of the growing season, both figures well above the norm of $5.50 per bushel. Even though less rain fell during April–June 1988 than fell during the drought that produced the Dust Bowl, farmers were not as devastated as they were in the 1930s, available quantities of grain from previous bumper crops allowing them to sell their surplus grain at a premium.

Some consider the drought of 1988 to be the worst natural disaster in U.S. history. While different parts of the country were enmeshed in drought from 1987 to 1989, the summer of 1988 stands out for a variety of reasons. The record low rainfall in the agricultural heartland of the country has already been pointed out. Overall, the United States was the driest it had been since 1895. Also, extremely high temperatures prevailed throughout the summer of 1988 in the Midwest and the Northeast, with many locations setting all-time records for June. Hundreds of deaths in cities such as Chicago and New York were attributed to the record heat. Nationwide, the heat and drought are credited with causing anywhere from five to ten thousand deaths, by far the most of any disaster in recent U.S. history. Hydrological problems included sinking water levels in wells, reservoirs, and rivers. For the entire period 1987–89, the country's total combined losses were estimated to be $39 billion.

On the basis of the drought indices, the 1988 drought was not as bad as the drought that produced the Dust Bowl, when the PDSI dropped to the range –7 to –8, and it was not as long as the severe drought of the 1940s, which lasted for 5 years in western Kentucky. However, it was followed within a decade by another period of severe to extreme drought conditions.

One of the major causes of the drought of 1999 was a persistent area of high pressure over the Midwest. This created conditions similar to those created by the weather patterns of 1988, for example, cutting off the flow of moisture from the Gulf of Mexico to Kentucky. Kentucky was already susceptible to drought, having experienced dry weather during the last half of 1998, and in 1999 several cities in the state had their driest summers on record. The peak impact of the drought statewide occurred over the period from August through October. At Louisville, the 3-month rainfall total for the period July–September was 2.01 inches, or 18% of normal. Lexington's total for the same period was only 4.67 inches, which broke a record for dryness set in 1903.

Heat waves during the summer months worsened the drought and caused many deaths. By the end of September, nearly 1 million

FIGURE 36. *Kentucky tobacco grower in a field of drought-damaged plants.*
(Louisville Courier-Journal.)

people had been affected by the drought, more than 400,000 of them facing some type of mandatory water conservation. Impacts were greatest in northern and southeast Kentucky. Farmers were badly hurt by the 1999 drought, with corn production down by about 10% from the 1998 level. The late-summer dryness particularly hurt soybean growers, who saw their crop reduced by about 40% from the previous year.

By the end of September, ninety-six of Kentucky's counties were under a water shortage warning, and the remainder were under a water shortage watch. Much of the fall rain in 1999 missed Kentucky, and the water deficits continued into the winter. By

November, fires had consumed eighty thousand acres statewide, prompting the governor to sign an executive order declaring a state of emergency. According to the state's Division of Forestry, twenty-five thousand acres burned between November 8 and November 15 alone. In early December, a water emergency continued for all or part of fifty-three counties, with water shortage warnings still covering another forty-three counties.

10

OTHER WEATHER
ELEMENTS

The environment of Kentucky is not measured in terms of temperature and precipitation alone. The comfort and especially the discomfort sensed depend on several interacting weather elements. Conditions can be hot and humid, cold and windy, and mild and sunny—any combination of which can determine how to dress for the day or how to plan for outdoor work. The wind, humidity, cloud cover, etc. can be equally dramatic and extreme in their effects, and no review of Kentucky's weather would be complete without considering them.

WIND

An area of high pressure that prevails off the southeastern coast of the United States for most of the year is a dominant factor in determining the wind patterns in Kentucky. The clockwise circulation of air around this high causes the southerly winds on its western edge that cover the region from the Gulf Coast to the Ohio River. Occasionally, cold fronts moving across the continent cause the winds to shift to a northerly direction, but the southerly winds usually return within a few days.

The long-term records indicate the remarkable persistence of the southerly winds at most locations in Kentucky, although a westerly component is also evident. During the late winter months—February and March—there is a tendency for northwesterly winds to predominate in a small area around Louisville. During the winter and early spring, when very active low-pressure systems are moving through Kentucky, winds are likely to be strongest. Daily average wind speeds at that time are about 10–12 mph. The summer months are usually more placid, and during that period average wind speeds are reduced to 6–8 mph.

In addition to the sustained winds, Kentucky also sees isolated brief gusts generated by thunderstorms. Gusts in excess of 80 mph have been reported by airport observation posts. Because observation stations equipped to make wind measurements are widely scattered, it is likely that stronger gusts, perhaps exceeding even 100 mph, occur and have simply gone unmeasured. This conjecture is supported by the fact that these gusts sometimes cause straight-line wind damage as severe as that caused by a small tornado, the hammer-like blow that they deliver (the combined effect of the strength of the gust and the speed with which it reaches its peak) uprooting trees, overturning mobile homes, and destroying barns.

Because pilots have the greatest need of up-to-date information about wind speed and direction, and because airports are usually constructed at sites where wind flow is unobstructed and, thus, representative of the general wind flow in the area, most wind data in Kentucky are collected at airports. Much of Kentucky is, however, characterized by irregular terrain. And, just as such irregular terrain can, as we have seen, create frost pockets, so too can it create variations in wind flow. For example, people living on the north or east side of a hill are sheltered from the prevailing winds and usually experience lesser average wind speeds. Similarly, those living in a valley between two knobs or small mountains usually experience greater average wind speeds owing to the channeling of the wind around the hills and through the gap.

Irregular terrain can also establish its own wind circulation because of uneven daytime heating effects. During the day, a south-facing slope will receive more sunlight and become warmer than the valley it overlooks. As the air closest to the ground on the sunlit hillside is heated and rises, a wind begins to blow gently up the slope. The wind throughout the nearby valley will begin to move in that direction. In the late afternoon, hillsides that are in shadow will begin to cool, and the air next to the ground will also be cooled. As the air cools, it becomes denser and begins to flow back down the slope, pulled by the force of gravity. The light wind that results can continue for much of the night and produce temperatures in the valley that are several degrees cooler than those at the top of the slope.

Increased emphasis on air quality in recent years has resulted in considerable interest in the connection between wind flow over and air pollution in large cities. During periods of light winds, the air over cities is essentially stagnant and, therefore, becomes laden with pollutants, the sources of which (automotive traffic, industrial plants, etc.) tend to concentrate in urban areas. The problem worsens when the air cannot mix vertically.

Normally, temperatures decrease as height above the ground increases, but there are some meteorological conditions under which the reverse occurs—notably at night when the ground cools under clear skies and the lowest 500 feet or so is colder than the overlying air, or sometimes when an approaching warm front causes warmer air to override cold air that is present near the surface. These reversed temperature conditions are called *inversions*, and the associated shallow layer of cold, dense air near the ground essentially forms a lid that limits the upward movement of air and, thus, any chance to disperse air pollutants.

Periods of stagnant air normally occur during the summer, when winds are lightest and weather systems move slowly. The prevalence of poor dispersion during the summer means that this is typically the time of year when most air-pollution episodes occur.

CLOUD COVER

The frequent low-pressure centers and the associated cold fronts that affect Kentucky bring considerable cloud cover to the state. Even during the periods between lows there is usually sufficient moisture for some degree of cloud cover to develop, if only a few cumulus clouds in midafternoon. Seldom does a day go by without some clouds being noticeable somewhere in the sky.

Cloud cover is measured in terms of the proportion of the sky that is obscured by clouds. At most airports, hourly observations are made of the extent of cloud cover as well as of the height and types of clouds present. From these observations, long-term averages of cloud cover can be calculated. Clouds are of most climatological interest because of their effect in curtailing sunshine. Therefore, summaries of the amount of cloud cover often show the amount during the period from sunrise to sunset separately. Across all of Kentucky, the average annual cloud cover ranges from 60% in the western part of the state to 70% in the northeast.

Even though the hills of eastern Kentucky apparently do not, as we have seen, enhance rainfall, there is typically more cloud cover in the northeastern part of the state. This is because there are more clouds formed when the moisture-bearing winds from the Great Lakes region occasionally flow southeast and are lifted over the Appalachian Mountains. That effect is maximized over western Pennsylvania, eastern Ohio, and northeastern Kentucky.

The seasonal variation in cloud cover reveals a maximum during the winter months, when about 65% of the sky is normally obscured during the day in western Kentucky and 75% in the northeast. During the summer months, the average cloud cover decreases to about 55% in western Kentucky and 60% in the east. For the entire state, cloud cover reaches a minimum of about 50%–55% during October, the driest month of the year.

SUNSHINE

Solar radiation, or sunshine, is the basic source of energy for many of the processes that go on around us, for example, the growth of plants, the heating of the air, and the evaporation of water. It is usually measured as the amount of energy that falls on a horizontal surface 1 centimeter square, or about the size of a side of a sugar cube, with energy expressed in terms of calories, a calorie being the amount of heat required to raise the temperature of 1 cubic centimeter of water by 1°C.

In order to determine the total amount of solar radiation that reaches the earth's surface, such factors as amount of cloud cover (which reflects solar radiation), latitude, and season of the year must be taken into consideration. If there were no clouds in the earth's atmosphere, an equal amount of solar radiation would be received at every point having the same latitude. Since cloud cover varies, both daily and seasonally, from one location to another, there is considerable variation in the amount of solar energy received at ground level.

Solar intensity is greatest when sunlight falls perpendicularly on a level surface. At the latitude of Kentucky, the sun never quite reaches directly overhead, and, consequently, its rays fall perpendicularly, and with maximum intensity, only on those surfaces tilted enough to compensate for its angle. The intensity of the solar energy reaching all other surfaces is reduced: the greater the departure from perpendicular, the lesser the intensity of the solar energy. The sloping hillsides in Kentucky are a good example of how the sun's energy varies in intensity. The south-facing slopes, which are tilted in such a way that they receive the rays of the sun more directly, are much warmer than the north-facing slopes, which receive the sun's rays less directly. In the springtime, grass, trees, and flowers are more advanced on the warmer, south-facing slopes.

In any study of climate, solar radiation must be measured on a horizontal surface in order to provide a uniform measurement from one location to another. Such measurements in and near Kentucky reveal that the greater cloud cover over the eastern sections of the state reduces the average radiation slightly below levels found in western Kentucky. However, observations of sufficient detail to allow any precise comparisons to be made are not available.

RELATIVE HUMIDITY

The predominantly southerly winds in Kentucky bring enough water vapor from the Gulf of Mexico to maintain a humid climate. During the summer months, winds will briefly become southwesterly, bringing with them a flow of drier air from the arid portions of the southern plains states. The flow of air across the

Great Lakes is primarily northwesterly during the winter, which makes them a source of moisture for the states to the north of Kentucky, but their effect is slight south of the Ohio River, mostly causing greater cloud cover.

Kentucky's lakes and major rivers cause some local variations in humidity level. Generally, however, the same humidity regime prevails statewide. This is due primarily to the fact that no section of the state lies close enough to the Gulf region to allow exposure to persistent ocean breezes.

Relative humidity is a gauge of the amount of water vapor in the air compared to the amount the air can possibly hold at the temperature it happens to be when measured. That is, it is a gauge of how close the air is to being saturated. As the air cools, it can hold less water, and so it comes closer to saturation, or 100% humidity. For a given amount of moisture droplets in the air, the relative humidity will be higher at night, when the temperature normally drops and brings the air to near its saturation point. The humidity will be highest around sunrise—normally around 90%. This brief period of high humidity is often accompanied by a light fog or haze that restricts visibility until temperatures begin to rise. Similarly, the relative humidity becomes lower when air is warmer and has the ability to hold more moisture. During the afternoon period, when temperatures are warmest, the humidity normally drops to the lowest levels of the day. In the winter, the lowest humidity of the day averages about 60%, while, in the spring and summer, the afternoon humidity will reach about 50%. On a few hot, dry days in midsummer, it is not unusual for the humidity to drop as low as 18%–20% during the afternoon. The mean relative humidity for the year averages close to 70%.

What makes summer days seem so uncomfortable if humidity is typically lower during the summer? The combination of heat and humidity. That is, a day with a relative humidity level of 50% will seem much more uncomfortable if temperatures climb into the 90°s than it will if they stay in the 70°s. To put it another way, as relative humidity increases, the air seems warmer than it actually is because the body is less able to cool itself via the evaporation of

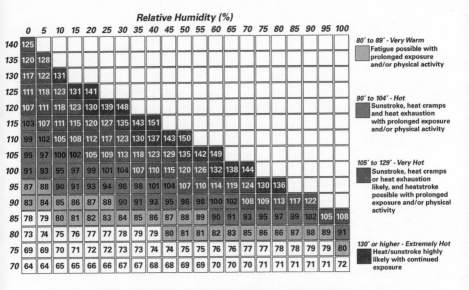

FIGURE 37. *National Weather Service heat index chart.*
(Data provided by National Weather Service.)

perspiration. The *heat index* measures the temperature that the body feels when the effects of heat and humidity are combined. A heat index of 70 or below is considered to be both comfortable and safe. As the heat index approaches 80, conditions begin to be uncomfortable, but they are still safe for most people. A heat index of 80 or more is not only uncomfortable but also dangerous, the more dangerous and the more uncomfortable the higher it rises. The precise effects of higher heat-humidity levels are outlined in figure 37.

In Kentucky, the heat index normally reaches or exceeds 79 about 500 hours a year in the western and south-central portions. That level is reached only about 200 hours per year in the north-eastern sections.

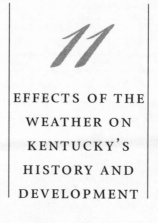

EFFECTS OF THE WEATHER ON KENTUCKY'S HISTORY AND DEVELOPMENT

The development of a region is determined by the resources available to the people who arrive there, and climate is a resource as surely as soils, trees, and minerals are. But climate is also more than just a resource in that it in fact determines what other resources a region has to offer. For example, fertile soils and large trees can develop only under certain weather conditions. Kentucky's distinctive climate has contributed to its distinctive development.

One of the best examples of the influence of climate on development is the state's bourbon whiskey industry. Bourbon whiskey, which is sold worldwide, is produced almost exclusively in Kentucky. The production method involves the distilled whiskey being placed into charred oak casks to age for several years in unheated warehouses, and distillers sometimes claim that essential to any good bourbon is its expansion and contraction inside the barrel. Kentucky's occasionally extreme summer heat expands the aging whiskey, pressing it into the charred oak of the cask, adding taste and color, and its occasionally frigid temperatures shrink the spirit, drawing it back out of the wood. As this cycle is repeated over several years, the product develops its unique characteristics.

The ample rainfall and moderate temperatures normally found in Kentucky have been ideal for the development of the state's agriculture industry. Most field crops grow best at temperatures between 60°F and 85°F, a range especially favorable for two of Kentucky's major plantings, corn and tobacco. In addition, the state's dependable late winter, early spring rainfall is stored in the soil, providing a bit of insurance against dryness in the summer growing season. That moisture is adequate in most years means that, unlike their counterparts in the Great Plains and dry western states, few Kentucky farmers need expensive irrigation systems.

Once farmers have their crops in the ground and growing well past midseason, their thoughts turn from water to frost. An early frost can kill a crop before it reaches maturity, and nothing is more distressing to Kentucky farmers than a field of tobacco hit by an early freeze. It turns as black as their hatbands and is worth about as much. The length of the freeze-free season in a region determines which crops can be profitably grown there. For example, the shortness of the growing season has prevented widespread cotton production in Kentucky. King cotton made millionaires of some Southern growers in just a few seasons during the early nineteenth century, and its production spread into the southern and western portions of Kentucky. Kentucky farmers at one time tried to grow cotton as far north and east as Campbellsville, but the average freeze-free season there is about 20 days shorter than the 200 days normally required to produce a cotton crop.

The crop that established the backbone of Kentucky's agriculture industry was tobacco, which does not require the long growing season that cotton does. The early settlers who came from Virginia and the Carolinas brought with them a knowledge of tobacco production, and they found the fertile soils well suited to tobacco's high nitrogen requirement. As soon as they had planted their corn crop—which by law they had to do in order to establish a claim to their homesteads—these early Kentuckians wasted no time in producing tobacco. The first boatload of tobacco was taken downriver to be sold in New Orleans in 1787.

The predominant type of tobacco grown in Kentucky is burley. Burley alone accounted for $518 million of the approximately $1.7 billion in crops produced statewide in 2000, and it constitutes about a third of tobacco production nationwide. Burley imparts flavor to tobacco products, and Kentucky produces some of the most desirable leaf in the country. Unfortunately for growers, it is sensitive to the weather because it is air cured. What this means is that, even after growers have harvested their burley, they are still far from the high-quality leaf desired at market and still at the mercy of the weather.

Kentucky is a leading producer of burley tobacco because it has the unique combination of soils and climate needed to give the burley the desirable quality. The most critical weather conditions occur during the curing period since they influence the chemical changes taking place—changes that ultimately produce the characteristic color, taste, and aroma of burley. The leaf alternately becomes soft and pliable during the damp mornings, then dry and brittle as the humidity drops in the afternoon. Farmers speak of tobacco coming in and out of *case*. The humidity in the curing barn must reach a level over 90% for the leaf to come into case and drop below 50% for it to go out of case. Each time the leaf goes in and out of case, it progresses further toward the finished tan product.

Gulf Coast and eastern seaboard states, where the humidity stays high in the afternoon, cannot produce a cured leaf of high quality. The weather there is too damp and, therefore, favors the development of mold, which farmers call *houseburn*, a problem that can substantially reduce the weight of the crop as well as its quality. Similarly, drier regions that do not have dependably high morning humidity cannot produce a successful cure either. The predictable product there would be a leaf with green or yellow mottling.

Of course, even in Kentucky not all days are favorable for the curing of burley, which is why curing barns are equipped with ventilators to control the air circulation and prevent moisture from building up. In order to help farmers obtain a better-quality cured leaf, the National Weather Service began in the mid-1950s to provide tobacco-curing advisories each day from August through November. These specialized forecasts—prepared by meteorologists first in Lexington, later in Louisville, and now back in Lexington at the University of Kentucky Agricultural

Weather Center—describe the humidity trends expected and the recommended curing practices for the next day or two.

One particularly important feature of the climate of Kentucky is that it provides the state's farmers with opportunities to produce multiple crops in the same field in the same year, a practice not normally possible in more northerly regions. For example, wheat or barley can be harvested in June or early July, and there is usually enough of the growing season left to plant a crop of soybeans in the stubble. The yield from late-planted soybeans is usually less than that from those that have grown a full season, but production is still adequate to be profitable. This particular double-cropping practice has been made possible by the development of new, small grain varieties that reach maturity earlier than do older varieties.

Weather has also historically favored the forest industry in Kentucky. As we have seen, the early settlers reported finding very large trees growing in the rich soil of their new home—oak, locust, and beech up to 5 feet in diameter, poplars 5–6 feet in diameter and over 100 feet tall. It took decades to clear the enormous timber from the state, with the last giants finally being felled from the hills of eastern Kentucky early in the twentieth century. Although the state does not today have a thriving timber industry, the climate still encourages the rapid growth of trees wherever the better soils are found. Unfortunately, the hills of eastern Kentucky, which are not suited to row crops, have thin, gravelly soils capable of holding little water. Otherwise, the ample rainfall in that region would make it one of the major hardwood-producing areas of the United States.

The water resources available have enabled Kentucky to develop the finest state park system in the United States. The terrain is particularly suited to the damming of streams, and rainfall is adequate to fill the reservoirs thereby created. The summer months see substantially more warm sunny days in Kentucky than they do in the northern states, which abound with natural lakes.

Even before the development of the state park system, however, Kentucky's climate lured vacationers. Beginning very early in the nineteenth century, resort hotels were built at many of the state's mineral springs, some large enough to accommodate as many as a thousand guests at a time. These spas often attracted Southerners, who would pack up their families and head north to escape the disease that was then endemic to the lower Mississippi Valley and the Gulf Coast states during the hot summer months and take advantage of the supposed curative power of mineral springs. To get to Kentucky, Southerners would usually travel by steamboat to Louisville, where they transferred to smaller packets for the trip up the Kentucky River. Daytime activities at the spas included tenpins, croquet, riding, "taking the waters"—and napping during the hottest part of the afternoon. Nighttime meant dancing and taking a stroll in the cool air.

The ties between Kentucky and the South were by the early nineteenth century already close since the Bluegrass region served as a source of blooded livestock for the plantations. But, despite these ties and the state's abundance of spas and enticingly temperate climate, what made Kentucky a particularly attractive destination for antebellum Southerners was that, unlike the other upper Midwest states boasting similar resorts and climates, Kentucky was a slave state—the Bluegrass region even maintained a flourishing slave trade alongside its livestock trade—and traveling to Kentucky did not mean risking losing slaves.

Many of the Kentucky spas closed during the Civil War. And, while the state's resort business recovered somewhat later in the century, it never regained its former glory. Part of the reason was that, no longer being able to own slaves, Southerners had no reason not to seek out even more temperate summers farther north. Travel by train had also become easier, and resorts in such faraway places as Atlantic City, Saratoga, and even Niagara Falls drew customers away from Kentucky.

The rivers that brought the Southern planters and their families to the spas also served as avenues for trade, development, and settlement. Kentucky's rivers first saw the rough rafts and keelboats of the early settlers, then the grand steamboats. In the early days before locks and dams made year-round navigation possible, the Ohio River rose and fell with the rains. By the early 1800s, many of the supplies and much of the news coming from the East traveled down the Ohio from Pittsburgh to Maysville, the gateway to the Bluegrass region; to Cincinnati; and to Louisville. It was not uncommon for the *Kentucky Gazette,* published in Lexington, to comment in late summer or fall that there was no news because a spell of dry weather had brought the river to a stage too low to be navigable.

Travel on the Ohio was also restricted in the winter because of its tendency to freeze over. Richard H. Collins's *History of Kentucky,* published in 1874, contains the following account:

> For ten days previous to Tuesday, December 20, 1796, the Ohio River had been frozen over to the depth of 9 inches, enclosing firmly the "Kentucky boats" of quite a number of emigrants. Heavy rains fell, inspiring them with hopes of release and of a prosperous journey; but the weather turned colder, and on that night, and the next, the thermometer stood at 17° below zero. Before daylight, on the 22nd, the ice bridge [probably an ice dam] broke up with a noise like thunder, carrying to destruction many of the boats, and to death some of their adventurous passengers.

The winter ice on the Ohio River must have been a greater threat to life than either the Indians, disease, or the privations of a frontier existence. The *Kentucky Gazette* carried this note on January 15, 1805, from Limestone, now known as Maysville: "13 boats lost on the Ohio River near Limestone by the ice." On February 5, we find this elaboration: "Accounts from the Ohio River represent the destruction of boats and lots of property by the ice as being very considerable. It is said that upwards of 200 crafts of various descriptions have passed the mouth of Kentucky in the cakes of ice; some of them having persons on board frozen to death." And, on February 15, the editor reported that, after the ice had finally broken on February 10, he saw descending amid the flows eight flatboats, four keelboats, ten ferryboats, sixty to eighty canoes, and one house. He also reported that three families from Virginia and Maryland on an overturned boat had been lost, bringing the total number of emigrants who had drowned in the treacherous icy water to thirty-one.

Freezing of the Ohio River in any particular year is problematic and is normally dependent on a prolonged period of extremely cold weather. Data on actual freezing instances are limited to the port of Cincinnati, where records go back to 1874. The U.S. Department of Commerce reports that the Ohio River at Cincinnati has frozen over in only fourteen of the winters on record. It is, however, likely that there have been more instances further up-river near Ashland and fewer cases downriver.

The last instances of the Ohio River freezing solid were during the consecutive winters of 1976–77 and 1977–78. In 1976–77, the Cincinnati area suffered through a chilling 28 days at or below 0°F. The weather station at the airport near Covington hit its record low of -25°F on January 18, 1977. Ice was reported to be 12 inches thick on the river. In 1978, cold temperatures were a factor, but they were not quite as low as they had been the year before. During this second winter, it was the massive amount of snow that caused the river to freeze.

The present system of locks and dams creates longer and deeper pools of water on the Ohio River, thus limiting the opportunity for the river to freeze. However, tributaries in Kentucky are likely to see frozen surfaces much more often.

In the nineteenth century, before the locks and dams were constructed, boatmen feared the breakup of the Ohio River because of the damage it could cause. The *Cincinnati Daily Commercial* recorded one of the more spectacular breakups after the river had been closed by ice for 53 days, reporting on February 25, 1856:

> The shores of Ohio and Kentucky have been for weeks united by a bridge of crystal strong enough for the passage of droves of cattle and ponderous wagons with their loads and teams. On Saturday it was evident that this phenomenon was about to be dissolved. The boats were immovably fixed to the shore, exposed to the combined fury of an avalanche and flood.

A little after eleven P.M. the ice started! The bells of all the steamers rung their wildest alarms.

The Licking River was rising with some rapidity and about ten A.M. large quantities of ice were forced against the Ohio. There it rolled and leaped and plunged and crushed with a moaning, grating noise until one P.M. when the brittle clasps of the Ohio were partially broken and loosened and the Licking poured forth an angry eruption which raged across the Ohio and spent its first fury on the boats lying at the foot of Walnut Street where it made half-a-dozen wrecks.

Singular weather events have also had significant effects on Kentucky history. Consider, for example, the September 1778 siege of Fort Boonesboro, on the Kentucky River. The Indian chief Black Fish and four hundred warriors had attacked the fort on September 11, hoping to destroy the settlement and take prisoners back to Ohio. The settlers, under the leadership of Daniel Boone, who could muster only fifty able riflemen, faced certain defeat. After an opening skirmish, the Indians laid siege to the fort and, under the cover of gunfire, began tunneling toward it from the protection of the riverbank. But the sound of digging could be heard over the gunfire, and, hoping to intercept the Indians, Boone ordered the settlers to begin tunneling out of the fort.

After seven days, the Indians intensified their attack and succeeded in setting ablaze the cabin roofs inside the fort. Water supplies were too limited for the settlers to do anything but watch in horror as the flames spread throughout the fort. Their last defense was about to collapse, and they awaited the Indians' final assault.

And then, miraculously, rain began to fall. The rain fell all night, putting out the fires, and continued the next day, increasing in intensity until the battlefield was hidden from view. That night, the settlers went to bed soaked and with little hope of seeing the next day, but the morning dawned clear and strangely still. The sounds of digging were gone; indeed, the heavy rain had collapsed the Indians' tunnel, which had come within 20 yards of the fort but now lay swimming in mud. The longest siege in Kentucky history had failed, the victim of an unseasonably heavy rain.

The state's earliest settlers homesteaded in log cabins, usually one- or two-room structures tightly fortified against Indian marauders. But, as the country grew safer, homes were built in two separate sections connected by a covered breezeway or "dogtrot"—a characteristically Southern style and one more suited to creature comforts. The dogtrot served effectively as an outdoor living room, offering protection from the summer sun but still allowing a cool breeze to pass through. Unlike their compatriots farther north, who designed their homes to keep out the cold, Kentuckians opted for an early form of air-conditioning to enhance their summer comfort.

Weather has also been a determining factor in the Kentucky Derby. The premier horse race in the United States since its founding in 1875, the derby is held at Churchill Downs in Louisville early each May. May being a characteristically wet month—normally it has measurable rain on 12 of its 31 days in Louisville—chances are good that derby day will see rain. Rain—or a lack thereof—determines track conditions. And track conditions can go a long way toward determining a winner, some horses running best on a fast, dry track, others on a wet, muddy one. A review of the weather records for the period 1875–2004 indicates that measurable rain fell on forty-nine of 130 race days, or 38%, a figure remarkably close to the 39% probability of rain on a May day in Louisville. How did this affect race outcomes?

There is, unfortunately, no easy answer to that question since rain does not necessarily rule out a fast track. As is shown in table 5—which summarizes track conditions on derby day over the entire history of the race—the track was characterized by fast footing on ninety of 130 race days, meaning that some rain fell on at least twelve of those ninety days. Of course, on some race days the effects of rain are unmistakable. For example, rain had to be a factor on May 11, 1918, when, on a track rated muddy after 2.31 inches of rain, Exterminator won with the longest odds in the starting field, returning his backers $61.20 on a $2.00 win ticket. Then

TABLE 5. SUMMARY OF TRACK CONDITIONS FOR KENTUCKY DERBY EVENTS, 1875–2004

TRACK CONDITION	NUMBER OF OCCURRENCES
Dusty	3
Fast	90
Good	12
Heavy	8
Muddy	7
Sloppy	4
Slow	6

again, on other race days the effects of even heavy rain can be negligible, as in 2004. The prerace favorite that year was the undefeated Smarty Jones. Of his previous six starts, five had been run on tracks rated fast. The day of the race, however, thunderstorms passed over the track, and by post time it had been rated sloppy, the worst condition the favorite had ever faced. Still, the mud didn't slow Smarty Jones down in the slightest as he led the field of the nation's finest 3-year-olds to the finish line and won by nearly three lengths.

Has the state's weather affected the personalities of its inhabitants? The stormy personality of Cassius M. Clay (1810–1903), one of the state's most prominent, if not controversial, politicians—an abolitionist reluctant to give up his own slaves and a leading figure in Abraham Lincoln's administration who also served as a Union major general in the Civil War—is probably the best test case. Certainly Clay died as he had lived, amid the storm. The Lexington historian William H. Townsend gives us this account of Clay's last day:

In the twilight of the evening of July 22, 1903, a devastating tornado suddenly struck the Bluegrass. It unroofed every barn on the Whitehall plantation [Clay's home]. The courthouse cupola and every church spire in nearby Richmond were demolished. Giant limbs from forest trees hurtled through the air like wisps of straw. . . . Over in Lexington china in closets were crushed by concussions like earthquakes. . . . A bolt of lightning struck the statue of Henry Clay standing on his tall pedestal in the Lexington Cemetery and hurled the head 140 feet to the ground. . . . Then, in less than a half hour, it was over. . . . The stars came out, the wind sank to a fresh gentle breeze and thunder and lightning ceased. Big Jim Bowlin, the old general's nurse and bodyguard, tiptoed into the sick room to blow out the light of the coal oil lamp as he usually did before the old general went to sleep. Tonight it was not necessary, the old general was already asleep . . . his last sleep, laying on his back with his favorite Bowie knife peeping out from under his big pillow, his pain wracked features now untroubled and serene. The restless violent storm spirit of the old lion of Whitehall had gone zealously forward to meet its maker in the mightiest tempest that Central Kentucky had ever known.

CLIMATE CHANGE AND VARIABILITY

How much would you pay to be able to see into the future? The ability to predict what the economy will do or when and where natural disasters will occur would make you the envy of all (not to mention rich in the bargain). While no crystal ball is surefire, the weather can be an economic indicator of sorts. Of course, weather prediction remains a less than perfect science. Still, temperature trends can be predicted 5–7 days in advance and precipitation 2–3 days in advance, and most often watches for flash floods or tornadoes can be given 2–3 hours in advance.

One way in which to predict long-term trends is to review historical weather records for clues to recurrent cycles or correlations. These clues can then be used to forecast whether an upcoming season will be wetter, drier, hotter, or colder than usual. The search for such trends has resulted in many different interpretations of the available data, so many, in fact, that there have been almost as many weather cycles identified as there are cycle hunters.

In their search for data to establish the history of the earth's climate, scientists have been able to gather fairly precise information by using sources such as tree rings, ocean sediment core samples, and fossils. What they have established, as we have seen, is that a cooling trend that began about 100 million years ago reached its climax 3 million years ago in the great ice age and that, since that time, there have alternated periods of warming and cooling, alternately melting and building up the glaciers. Specifically, there

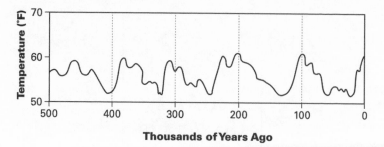

FIGURE 38. *Mean global temperature during the past 500,000 years.*
(Data provided by National Academy of Science.)

appears to have been a regular, although not precise, oscillation of the temperature through a range of about 10°F.

The last glacial period ended 10,000–20,000 years ago and was followed by a sharp rise in the mean global temperature. Our current civilization, which has enjoyed the fruits of plenty associated with a highly developed agricultural economy, has also enjoyed some of the warmest weather in the past 100,000 years. The highest temperature of this present interglacial period was reached about 6,000 years ago, and the climate has cooled slightly since that time. It has been estimated that a general cooling of 7°F–9°F below the current average would be sufficient to renew continental glaciation.

As we look for signs of temperature trends indicative of very-long-term fluctuations, we should keep in mind that the causes of variations are not necessarily the same today as they were even 25,000 years ago. There are many possible causes for cooling and warming trends, including slight changes in the earth's orbit, changes in the energy output of the sun, and changes in the balance between incoming and outgoing radiation. Today, an additional change has occurred that affects the radiation balance—a sharp increase in greenhouse gases. The greenhouse effect is a natural phenomenon—the trapping by atmospheric gases of some of the earth's heat—that helps regulate the temperature of the planet. There are a number of gases in the atmosphere that

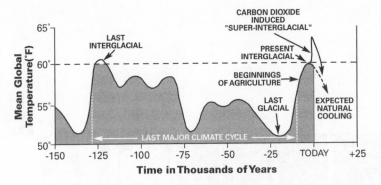

FIGURE 39. *Mean global temperature during the past 150,000 years.*
(Data provided by Department of Commerce.)

contribute to the greenhouse effect, but the most important are water vapor and carbon dioxide.

The carbon dioxide contained in our atmosphere is a by-product of fuel burning by our industrialized society. Since 1950, the amount of carbon dioxide measured in the atmosphere has grown by about 4% per year, and carbon dioxide is a gas that remains in the atmosphere for decades. Over the past 100 years, the global average temperature has increased by about 1°F, while at the same time there has been an expansion of the world economy and large increases in the burning of fossil fuels and, thus, the release of carbon dioxide. If we assume that such heightened levels of carbon dioxide in the atmosphere are, in fact, unprecedented, then it is more than likely that the present interglacial warm spell will be pushed to levels higher than those seen by any interglacial warm spell in the last 100,000 years. Some scientists predict that average global temperatures will increase by as much as 2°F–6°F by 2100. The consequences of such an increase would include changes in sea level and changes in global weather patterns, including more extreme weather.

Changes in world temperature cause changes in world pressure and wind patterns and, thus, changes in world precipitation patterns. What that means is that, if we can predict coming temperature changes, we might also be able to predict and, thus, prepare

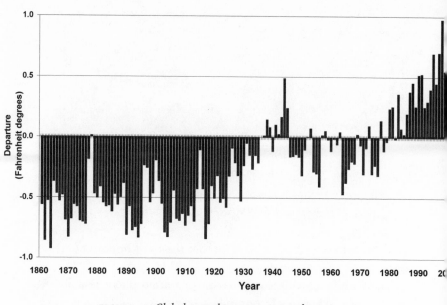

FIGURE 40. *Global annual temperature trends, 1861–2003.*
(Hadley Centre for Climate Prediction
and Research, United Kingdom Met Office.)

for the effects of global warming. This is not as impossible a job as it might sound. Scientists are using larger and faster computers to better simulate the effect of global warming on weather systems and the resulting precipitation patterns. This can give us a head start when it comes to taking whatever precautions turn out to be necessary, precautions that could range from developing plans to alleviate coastal flooding to developing new plant hybrids that are better adapted to a warmer or drier climate.

When it comes to actual expected effects of global warming, some scientists argue that increased levels of carbon dioxide in the atmosphere could be beneficial for plants generally and crops in particular, the carbon dioxide acting as a natural fertilizer. But plant growth is affected by many factors, including the temperature increases that go hand in hand with increased levels of carbon dioxide. While modest temperature increases are likely to enhance plant growth, significant temperature increases are more likely to inhibit it (absent the development of new hybrids). Rising temperatures will also increase the rate of evaporation, drying out the soils and, thus, stressing plants to such a degree that they die.

The key to making the best use of weather or climatic information is the determination of mathematical relations between weather and certain outcomes. One of the best examples is taking what we already know about the relation between weather and crop yields and applying it to expected future climates in order to determine the kinds of changes in food production that it will be necessary to make. It has been determined, for example, that the amount of moisture available during the month of July can explain most of the variability in the final yield of the Kentucky corn crop. That knowledge, coupled with predictions of coming changes in rainfall patterns, will allow scientists to predict, and thus prepare for, the effect of those changes on final corn crop production.

Scientists have, in fact, already used weather information in just this way. In 1973, when the United States was considering developing a supersonic transport aircraft, part of the planning process included taking account of the effect of expected contrails on crop production. It was determined that the high levels of contrail-produced cloud cover caused by the number of flights that these aircraft would have to make in order for the project to be a worthwhile investment would significantly reduce the amount of sunlight reaching the ground. The result would be notably cooler temperatures that would effectively halt corn production across the northern United States—one of the reasons the project was abandoned.

If it turns out that future climates can be expected to be less dependable than they are today, there will be an even greater need than there is today to control them artificially. A technology that has been in development since World War II—the artificial seeding of clouds to enhance or induce precipitation—will likely prove very important indeed. Of course, that technology will be most usefully employed in conjunction with what we already know about crop-weather relations. For example, the previously mentioned studies identifying the periods during which rainfall is critical to the Kentucky corn crop could be employed to determine exactly when clouds should be seeded.

Not just farmers, however, but people from all walks of life will benefit if we can increase our knowledge of future climate. Public policy is already being affected, forced as it is to grapple with such issues as the effect of air pollution on global temperatures. It should not, therefore, be surprising that considerable resources are being devoted to understanding climate change, an effort that has been immeasurably aided by the tremendous amounts of data that have become available recently, not to mention the new larger and faster computers that allow the more efficient processing of those data. There is still no widely accepted theory explaining the climate changes that are being observed, but most meteorologists agree that change is occurring and that the causes need to be well understood if we are to make intelligent choices for the future.

Particularly helpful to the effort to understand future climates is the growing body of knowledge about phenomena such as El Niño and La Niña that cause predictable changes in weather patterns. El Niño is an irregularly occurring flow of unusually warm surface water along the western coast of South America, La Niña an irregularly occurring flow of unusually cold surface water in the same place. Both cause global changes in weather patterns. For example, El Niño brings increased storm activity to the Pacific, which affects the jet stream, which affects the progression of high- and low-pressure systems across the United States.

Scientists have for some time now been monitoring sea-surface temperatures in the Pacific Ocean for signs that an El Niño or a La Niña event is developing. Recognizing such an event allows seasonal outlooks to be issued alerting people to significant departures from characteristic weather conditions. Typical users of this

TABLE 6. CHANGES FROM NORMAL KENTUCKY WEATHER DURING EL NIÑO OR LA NIÑA EVENTS

SEASON	EL NIÑO	LA NIÑA
Fall	Indeterminate	Warmer, wetter
Winter	Warmer	Warmer, wetter
Spring	Wetter	Warmer
Summer	Indeterminate	Indeterminate

type of information include water resource planners, energy companies, and emergency managers.

Meteorologists have compared Kentucky weather during the El Niño and La Niña events with normal conditions. What they have learned is that these Pacific Ocean anomalies do, in fact, affect the state's climate during certain seasons of the year. Table 6 shows some of these modifications. The comparison conditions in table 6 are long-term seasonal averages, which means that not all weather extremes are necessarily El Niño or La Niña related. Still, the comparisons are instructive—and cautionary.

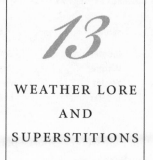

13

WEATHER LORE
AND
SUPERSTITIONS

One of the notable characteristics of Kentucky's climate is, as we have seen, its changeability—not just the variety of the seasons, but dramatic changes from day to day. The state was widely settled and the residents accustomed to the unexpected changes in the weather long before daily weather forecasting came into being. During the early period of Kentucky's history, it was common for Kentuckians to look to nature for signs that would help them predict the severity of the weather that was to come.

There is nothing uniquely Kentuckian about these signs and their associated superstitions. They were simply part of the folkways that the settlers brought with them. Perhaps the isolation of the Appalachian region or the strength of tradition in the state caused weather lore to persist more strongly in Kentucky than in some other states. Regardless of its origin or the reason for its persistence, however, some of that weather lore has proved surprisingly accurate—and some less so.

One traditional method of weather prognostication that continues to be popular today despite its demonstrated unreliability is the use of key, or control, days to forecast long-term weather trends. The most widely known of these is February 2, Groundhog Day, known in England as Candlemas Day. If on February 2 the sun shines bright enough to cast a shadow at any point during the day, there is an extended period of cold weather still to come. As an old English saying put it: "If Candlemas Day be fair and clear, there'll be two winters in the year." American lore employs a forecaster in the person of the groundhog, who on emerging and seeing his shadow instinctively returns to his den for an additional 6 weeks of hibernation. In Kentucky, only the period between 11:00 A.M. and 1:00 P.M. is considered to be significant on Groundhog Day.

Various regional variations on the tradition exist worldwide. In Germany the forecaster is the badger and in France the bear. Probably it was farmers who harbored the most interest in the chances that the winter would be an extended one, critical supplies likely running low by the beginning of February. As the old saying went: "Half the wood and half the hay, you should have on Candlemas Day." Just for insurance.

In Europe, the various saints' days were widely accepted as important weather control days. The best known was probably Saint Swithin's Day, which falls on July 15. Rain on Saint Swithin's Day foretold 40 more days of rain. For some reason—perhaps previous experience—40 days seems to appear regularly in connection with the various saints' days. For example, if it rains on Saint Medard's Day (June 8), it will rain again 40 days later, and, if it rains on Saint Protasius's Day (June 19) or Saint Bartholomew's Day (August 24), it will rain for 40 days.

Some of the key or control days are variable, not fixed. For example, according to one rule, the date of the first snowfall foretells the number of snows during the winter ahead. According to another, the number of fogs in August foretells the number of heavy snows to be expected over the course of the coming winter. And there are others: The first killing frost will come just 3 months after the katydids begin to chirp. The sound of thunder in February foretells a freeze (sometimes snow) in May. If it freezes on February 22, there will be forty more freezes (yet another forty!). If it snows on the first day of March, there will be snow for 30 days. Mists in March mean frost in May. If there is enough rain on Easter Sunday to wet a pocket handkerchief, it will be a good crop year.

The most powerful of all control days are supposed to be the 12 days following Christmas, which predict the weather for the following year. If December 26 is cold and snowy, then January will be cold and snowy. If December 27 is warmer than normal, then February will be warmer than normal. And so on. An alternative form of this tradition holds that the first 12 days of January foretell the year's weather.

Another traditional method of weather forecasting is to watch the changing signs of nature. Kentuckians seem particularly pre-occupied with predicting the severity of the coming winter. They watch animals, plants, insects, and even the moon closely, hoping for insight.

The woolly worm's stripes have long been considered portents of the coming winter's intensity. A wide black band is thought to indicate a bad winter. The greater the amount of black in proportion to the brown in the coat, the worse the winter will be. A brown band at both ends with an orange stripe in the middle indicates that the winter will be a mild one, a black stripe behind that the worst weather is past, and a black stripe in front that the worst is yet to come.

Animals are also watched for signs that they are preparing for winter's storms. When a cold winter is on the way, squirrels are supposed to grow bushier tails and begin gathering a large store of nuts early, and horses and other animals are supposed to grow thicker coats. Another indicator of cold weather is a cat sitting with its back to the fire.

Plants are supposed to give similar signs. Thick husks on corn mean cold weather ahead. As the old saying goes: "When the corn wears a heavy coat, so must you." In some areas, the onion fore-tells the winter: "Onion skins very thin, mild winter's coming in. Onion skins very tough, winter's going to be very rough." Other signs of a cold winter are hickory nuts dropping early, an early fall of leaves, and pinecones opening early. If grapes, apples, or cock-leburs mature early, an unusually hard winter is indicated.

No one has ever found real evidence that such methods have any real predictive power even a day ahead, much less a season. In fact, such characteristics of plants as thick husks on corn are de-termined by the past growing season's weather—by temperatures and moisture levels at critical growth stages, not by the weather that lies ahead.

Still, some weather lore does have a basis in fact. The changing appearance of the sky, rising humidity, shifting winds, and falling pressure have for centuries been perceived as signs of a change in the weather, accurate predictors identified long before the science of meteorology was born. According to Ben Franklin, one of this nation's earliest weather enthusiasts: "Know the signs of the sky, and you will far happier be."

Common for centuries among seamen has been the saying: "Red sky at morning, sailors take warning. Red sky at night, sailors delight." Or, as early Kentucky pioneers modified it: "Red sky at morning, travelers take warning. Red sky at night, travelers delight." Today we know that it is the clear skies that accompany the high-pressure centers moving across the country that cause the sun to appear brilliant red when it is low on the horizon in the morning or evening. A red rising sun is a warning sign because it indicates that a high-pressure center has passed, likely to be followed by a low-pressure center and stormy weather. A red setting sun is a delightful sign because it indicates that the high pressure is still to the west, likely to bring fair weather as it passes.

Then there's the rhyme about grazing cattle: "Tails to the east—weather's least. Tails to the west—weather's best." And it's true. Because grazing cattle instinctively turn their tails into an uncomfortable wind, a look across a pasture on a blustery day is as good as a look at a weather vane. Winds circulate counterclockwise around the low-pressure centers that bring stormy, or "least," weather. Because many of these systems develop in Texas, Oklahoma, or Arkansas and create easterly or southeasterly winds across Kentucky, cattle grazing with their tails to the east foretell an oncoming storm. After these low-pressure systems pass over Kentucky, the wind shifts back to the west, bringing a clearing trend. Thus, cattle grazing with their tails to the west foretell an approaching clear spell.

Passing pressure systems give other signs of weather changes. For example, pressure change can produce aches and pains and other physical symptoms in some people. The most common symptom is an aching in broken bones long mended. And that aching can be explained by even slightly falling pressure causing any air trapped in the knitted fracture to expand and press painfully on the bone.

Odors too are common signs of a change in the weather, always seeming more pronounced before a rain. Coal miners, for example, associate the smell of mine gas with oncoming rain or snow—for good reason. Because air moves from high pressure to low, a rapid drop in local atmospheric pressure will cause the air inside the mine to move outward, carrying its distinctive odor with it. In turn, the high pressure associated with fair weather traps the air in the mine, with the result that mine odors are much less readily apparent. The English have a saying about odors that goes: "Drains, ditches, and dunghills are more offensive before rain."

Passing pressure systems also bring with them fluctuations in humidity, which is lowest during fair weather and highest during foul. Humidity rises over the 6–12 hours before a rainstorm, causing characteristic signs to appear. Because certain fibers are sensitive to the moisture in the air, damp, humid weather can bring problems. Human hair becomes unmanageable. Ropes kink and twist. Because farmers do not like to cut their hay only to have it rained on, they look to the behavior of rope for a sign of coming inclement weather: "When ropes twist, forget your haying." But humidity affects more than just fibers. Cooks feel that humid weather is a bad time to make candy. As the saying goes: "If candy will not get hard, there will be rain."

Of course, modern scientific methods of weather forecasting are what most people rely on nowadays. Still, come fall, there will always be the urge to look up old-timers to read the signs. The hope is for a pleasant surprise and a mild winter. But, more likely than not, the forecast will be of a hard one.

The urge to exaggerate has always been particularly Kentuckian. Some Kentucky weather stories are so obviously exaggerated that the exaggeration, and not the weather anecdote, is clearly the point. Such is the encounter of a New Orleans editor with a Kentucky summer (quoted in Arthur Moore's 1959 *The Frontier Mind*): "I was once traveling in the state of Kentucky. It was summer and the heat of the sun is so great there at that season, that blacksmiths dispense altogether with coal, and heat their iron by a few minutes exposure to its rays."

Exaggeration can also be a way of dealing with hard times—humorously rather than bitterly. Certainly, the early Kentucky settlers who lived through the winter of 1779–80, one of extreme cold and hardship, took that approach. It was written that the weather became so cold that settlers out cutting firewood had to heat their axes before starting to chop on a tree; otherwise, they snapped like glass on striking a log.

One diary records it was so cold that "Miz Lawthorn," evidently a lady addicted to loud and excessive elocution, "frostbit her tongue while calling to a neighbor in the next house." The same writer says that trees exploded in the night with the sound of cannons as the sap froze and expanded in the bitter temperatures. In the same vein, he wrote that it was so cold that "sounds froze solid and an assortment of calf bawls, wolf howls, etc. could be seen rolling around over the snow." Another story tells of a settler who, because his family was facing starvation, went hunting in the frigid weather. He found no meat, but he did come back with a bag of frozen turkey gobbles, from which was made a nourishing broth.

Regardless of their authenticity or accuracy, Kentucky weather lore and proverbs undeniably add color to the oral traditions of the Bluegrass State. Just as colorful are the variations in the seasons—visible signs of the variety of a climate that invigorates the spirit. Ever perplexing, ever awesome, sometimes deadly, but never dull—the weather of Kentucky.

14

WEATHER
SERVICES IN
KENTUCKY

Basic weather services in Kentucky are provided by the National Weather Service (NWS). The NWS is part of the National Oceanic and Atmospheric Administration (NOAA), itself an agency of the U.S. Department of Commerce. It alone has the responsibility to issue regular weather forecasts, severe-weather warnings, and flood forecasts. However, there are a variety of other agencies and organizations that support the wide range of weather information and specialized services in the state.

WEATHER FORECASTS

The first proposal to create a national weather service was discussed in Congress in 1869. In 1870, Congress passed a resolution requiring the secretary of war to establish a government meteorological service—the Weather Bureau—within the War Department. The resolution provided for meteorological observations to be made at all military installations, where, it was argued, such an operation would be cheaper and military discipline would ensure that observations were, in fact, made. The establishment of the Weather Bureau within the War Department also meant access to a reporting system via the Army Signal Service's Division of Telegrams and Reports, to which the Weather Bureau was appended. The first official weather reports were sent by telegraph to Washington on November 8, 1870, and a storm warning was issued for the Great Lakes on the same day.

Weather services in Kentucky began on September 11, 1871, in

Louisville, where U.S. Army personnel made official weather observations. The first Signal Corps observer in Kentucky was Sergeant Thomas J. Brown, who reported for duty in Louisville on September 10, 1871. Brown set up his instruments in the Customs House at the corner of Third and Green Streets and telegraphed the first report to Washington the next day. He was the first of a dozen army noncommissioned officers to command the Louisville office.

At first, the primary purpose of the Weather Bureau was issuing storm warnings for shipping on the Great Lakes, the Gulf Coast, and the Atlantic seaboard. Soon, however, more farmers than sailors were using the weather information that it provided, so, in 1891, the Weather Bureau was transferred to the Department of Agriculture. Sergeant Frank Burke, who had taken command at Louisville in 1887, exchanged his uniform for civilian clothes and became the first civilian chief of the Kentucky weather office.

The Army Signal Service opened a second weather office in Kentucky in 1887 at Lexington. Prior to that, weather observations had been taken at the state college for a short period (1872–76). Both the Louisville and the Lexington offices operated continuously through the 1920s. But a reduction in services during the Depression forced the closure of the Lexington office in 1933. When a second Weather Bureau office was reestablished in Kentucky in 1944, it was at the Lexington airport, Blue Grass Field, for the purpose of taking aviation weather observations and disseminating forecasts.

The Louisville office, located in the downtown area, was responsible for all forecasts and warnings to the public throughout Kentucky. Initially, the forecasts were released to the local newspapers and distributed statewide by telegraph. Later, they were disseminated to the press wire services, which relayed them to newspapers, radio, and television throughout the state.

The office staff was responsible for preparing forecasts and also making the official weather observations for the city. It was also responsible for gathering weather observations from over fifty volunteer weather observers scattered throughout the state.

A second, satellite Weather Bureau office was opened at Bowman Field, 5.5 miles east–southeast of the city center in 1930. That office became the place where aviation observations were made, the staff there being easily accessible to the growing aviation industry, which was highly dependent on weather information.

Opening a weather station at Bowman Field was indicative of coming changes in the nation's weather services, changes meant to provide better information for airplane pilots. In 1940, the Weather Bureau, as a government agency, was again transferred, this time from the Department of Agriculture to the Department of Commerce, where its companion agency was the Civil Aviation Authority, another nod to the growing importance of the aviation industry.

Beginning July 1, 1945, Bowman Field was made the official weather-observing site for the city of Louisville, leaving only the forecasting program in the downtown office. Then, on December 1, 1947, the Weather Bureau personnel and the observing program at Bowman Field were all moved to Standiford Field, about 4 miles south–southeast of the city center. In 1955, the downtown office was closed, and the state forecasting program was consolidated with the observing program at Standiford Field.

Moving all the Louisville Weather Bureau functions to Standiford Field indicated the growing importance of that airport, which was fast becoming the hub for commercial airline service in Louisville and the lower Ohio Valley. By that point, Weather Bureau offices had been established at airports in nearby Cincinnati, Ohio, and Evansville, Indiana, and given forecast responsibility for a few counties in Kentucky that were within their larger metropolitan areas. However, the main forecast responsibility for most of the state remained with the Louisville office, now at Standiford Field.

In 1970, President Richard Nixon established NOAA as a way to bring together many of the science-based agencies that had responsibility for activities such as ocean surveys, fisheries, and weather forecasting. In the reorganization that followed, the Weather Bureau was transferred to NOAA and renamed the National Weather Service.

FIGURE 41. *Areas of responsibility in Kentucky for NWS forecast offices.*
(National Weather Service.)

Changes in weather-forecasting responsibilities in Kentucky began in 1981, when the NWS installed new offices at Jackson, to serve the eastern part of the state, and at Paducah, to serve the western section. With the exception of a few counties in the north and northeast parts of the state served by the NWS offices in Wilmington, Ohio, and Charleston, West Virginia, the Louisville, Paducah, and Jackson offices cover the entire state between them—and then some (see figure 41).

Each of the forecast offices is staffed with a full complement of meteorologists and other specialists needed to operate the facilities. Doppler weather radars and satellite-receiving systems in the offices provide real-time information with which to prepare forecasts and issue weather warnings.

Prior to the modernization program, many weather offices were, as we saw in the case of the Bowman Airport office, located in airport operations centers or terminal buildings, easily accessible to airplane pilots. Today, however, NWS offices are more likely to be located in their own buildings, ones specially designed to accommodate the radar and other electronic equipment that

FIGURE 42. *The NWS office at Paducah. Note the tower for Doppler weather radar behind the building.* (National Weather Service.)

modern weather forecasting requires. These NWS offices produce standard forecast products, including public forecasts for specific areas (groups of four to ten counties with usually similar weather conditions), aviation forecasts of flying conditions, fire weather forecasts, and air-stagnation advisories. They must also issue watches and warnings—for winter storms, severe thunderstorms, tornadoes, and floods—as needed.

NOAA WEATHER RADIO

NOAA Weather Radio (NWR) is a nationwide network of radio stations broadcasting continuous weather information directly from a nearby NWS office. NWR broadcasts warnings, watches, forecasts, and other hazard information 24 hours a day. It is an "all-hazards" radio network, making it a singular source for comprehensive weather and emergency information.

Known as the "Voice of the NWS," NWR is provided as a public service. The system includes more than 670 transmitters, covering

TABLE 7. LOCATIONS AND FREQUENCIES OF NOAA WEATHER RADIO STATIONS BROADCASTING IN KENTUCKY

EASTERN KENTUCKY		CENTRAL KENTUCKY		WESTERN KENTUCKY	
LOCATION	FREQUENCY	LOCATION	FREQUENCY	LOCATION	FREQUENCY
Somerset	162.550	Lexington	162.400	Mayfield	162.475
Ashland	162.550	Covington	162.550	Madisonville	162.525
Mount Vernon	162.425	Bowling Green	162.400	Hopkinsville	162.450
London	162.475	Elizabethtown	162.550	Whitesville	162.475
Williamsburg	162.500	Owenton	162.450		
Monticello	162.425	Maysville	162.425		
Hazard	162.475	Burkesville	162.475		
Pikeville	162.400	Campbellsville	162.525		
Paintsville	162.525	Ekron	162.450		
Jackson	162.425	East Madison County	162.525		
McKee	162.450	West Madison County	162.525		
Manchester	162.400	Madison County	162.525		
Pineville	162.525	Horse Cave	162.500		
Harlan	162.450				
Phelps	162.500				
Beattyville	162.500				
Morehead	162.425				
Stanton	162.550				
Frenchburg	162.475				
West Liberty	162.450				

all fifty states, adjacent coastal waters, Puerto Rico, the U.S. Virgin Islands, and the U.S. Pacific Territories. Listening to NWR requires a special radio receiver or scanner capable of picking up the signal. The range of a typical NWR station is generally about 40 miles, but it can be less in mountainous terrain.

Kentucky was the first state to develop a plan for full statewide coverage by the NWR system. In the 1970s, the Kentucky educational television network had an existing network of broadcast towers to which separate antennas could be attached for the individual NWR stations. A total of thirty-seven installations currently exist, allowing everyone in the state to receive current weather forecasts and warnings. A list of the stations and their operating frequencies is given in table 7.

The information broadcast continuously on the NWR system includes:

- *the regional weather synopsis:* a summary of the weather for the next 12–24 hours across the Ohio and Tennessee Valleys, including Kentucky and Indiana;
- *the local 5-day forecast:* covering the NWR listening area in question;
- *the hourly weather roundup:* a summary of the current weather conditions for cities across Kentucky and surrounding states;
- *the "NOWCast":* a short-term forecast valid for the next 6 hours and updated as often as necessary to reflect changing weather conditions;
- *climatic information:* including temperatures, precipitation amounts, and climate normals; and
- *river summaries:* including stage and forecast information for major rivers as well as other reservoir and lake data.

Other information is broadcast as needed:

- *public information statements:* which give extra information, such as weather-safety tips or hazardous-driving statements; and
- *severe-weather watches, warnings, and advisories:* which relay information regarding the location and movement of severe storms.

WEATHER-OBSERVATION PROGRAM

Weather forecasts and warnings can be no better than the weather observations that are available. A weather observation can be as simple as a reading of the daily rainfall amount or as complex as an hourly aviation report, which includes data on such elements as cloud height, visibility, and the current altimeter setting. The three NWS offices in Kentucky by themselves are not adequate to define the weather systems that are affecting the state or provide the data that are needed as input to the weather-forecasting models being run on large computers. Therefore, there are several additional weather-observation programs active in the state providing input to many different types of weather-forecasting programs.

The surface weather observations used for basic forecasting are normally made at least once each hour so that they collectively create a snapshot of current weather systems affecting the country. Since aviation is a major user of weather observations, most hourly observations are made today at airports. Ever since the days when the Weather Bureau and the Civil Aviation Agency were Commerce Department companions—the Civil Aviation Agency has since become the Federal Aviation Administration and been transferred to the Department of Transportation—the aviation community has been a faithful supplier of weather observations. For many years, aviation weather observations were made by trained weather-service and aviation-agency observers who read the instruments at their airports and made visual estimates of cloud cover and visibility. A modernization program started in the 1980s developed an automated weather-observing system using modern computer technology and remote-sensing instruments.

The Automated Surface Observing Systems (ASOS) program has been a joint effort of the NWS, the Federal Aviation Administration, and the Department of Defense. ASOS serves as the nation's primary surface-weather-observing network. ASOS is designed to support weather-forecasting activities and aviation operations and, at the same time, the needs of the meteorological, hydrological, and climatological research communities.

Additionally, ASOS routinely provides computer-generated voice observations directly to aircraft in the vicinity of airports, using ground-to-air radio. These messages are also available via a telephone dial-in port. ASOS observes, formats, archives, and transmits observations automatically. And it transmits a special report when conditions exceed preselected weather-element thresholds, for example, when visibility decreases to less than 3 miles.

ASOS routine reports include the following basic weather elements:

- *sky condition:* cloud height and amount (clear, scattered, broken, overcast) up to 12,000 feet;

- *visibility* (to at least 10 statute miles);
- *basic present-weather information:* type and intensity of rain, snow, and freezing rain;
- *obstructions to vision:* fog, haze;
- *pressure:* sea-level pressure, altimeter setting;
- *ambient temperature, dew-point temperature;*
- *wind:* direction, speed, and character (gusts, squalls);
- *precipitation accumulation;* and
- *selected significant remarks:* including variable cloud height, variable visibility, precipitation beginning/ending times, rapid pressure changes, pressure-change tendency, wind shift, peak wind.

The current and most recent weather observations from ASOS are available on the Internet via links found on the homepage for each of the NWS offices. The ASOS weather stations operating in Kentucky are listed in table 8. Additional ASOS stations operate at locations in states near Kentucky. These include Cape Girardeau, Missouri; Huntington, West Virginia; and Evansville, Indiana.

Weather radar is another important observing tool that is available to forecasters in the NWS offices. Radar was initially developed for such military applications as detecting airplanes and ships. However, developments in radar technology since World War II have created systems that can be optimized to detect weather elements such as rain, hail, and snow.

By the 1980s, developments in weather-radar technology included the use of Doppler techniques to detect the movements of precipitation particles that alert meteorologists to conditions associated with tornadoes and destructive winds. The intensity of the radar return also indicates whether damaging hail might be present in a particular thunderstorm. The NWS has installed a national network of Doppler weather radars. The military services have installed similar weather radars at several of their installations around the country, and they contribute their information to the national radar network.

TABLE 8. AUTOMATED SURFACE WEATHER STATIONS OPERATING IN KENTUCKY

WESTERN KENTUCKY	CENTRAL KENTUCKY	EASTERN KENTUCKY
Paducah	Louisville Bowman Field	London
Owensboro	Louisville Standiford Field	Jackson Carroll Field
Fort Campbell	Covington	London
	Frankfort	Somerset
	Fort Knox	
	Bowling Green	

Weather radars have become valuable tools for issuing timely severe-weather warnings. Doppler weather radars are operated by the NWS at each of its offices in Paducah, Louisville, and Jackson. Additionally, a Doppler weather radar operates at the Fort Campbell army post near Hopkinsville and adds information about weather occurring in that part of the state.

COOPERATIVE WEATHER OBSERVATIONS

An even denser network of weather observers is needed to aid the NWS in its flood-forecasting program and to provide climate information. There are about a hundred cooperative weather-observing stations in the state where volunteers make daily observations of elements such as precipitation, maximum/minimum temperature, and river stage. The NWS tries to maintain at least one cooperative observer in each county, and some of the observing locations have been in existence for over 100 years. Some of the cooperative stations are government facilities, such as Corps of Engineers' dams or agricultural experiment station farms, but many are manned by average citizens who serve without pay, faithfully recording and reporting the readings from instruments provided to them by the NWS.

The cooperative observer reports are archived at NOAA's National Climatic Data Center at Asheville, North Carolina. Monthly reports are issued that include the readings made and reported by the cooperative observers throughout the state. Copies of the monthly reports are available for purchase and are often used in climate studies by engineers and planners. The legal community is

FIGURE 43. *Cooperative weather observer
Bennie Kessler at Lebanon, Kentucky.*

also a major user of the weather-observation records because they
can be critical evidence in certain types of litigation.

RIVER AND FLOOD FORECASTS

River and stream forecasts are important parts of the service that
is provided by the NWS. Heavy rainfall or snow melt running into
the Ohio River and its tributaries in Kentucky can create the potential for serious flooding. The NWS prepares routine river-stage

forecasts using daily precipitation reports from cooperative observers and automated rain gauges. The Wilmington, Ohio, River Forecast Center has the responsibility for providing major flood guidance for the Ohio River and its tributaries in Kentucky down to Kentucky Lake. The lower Mississippi River Forecast Center in Slidell, Louisiana, provides forecast guidance for the tip of Kentucky that is west of Kentucky Lake.

Guidance forecasts from these river centers are sent daily to each of the three NWS forecasting offices in Kentucky. Specialists in these offices must monitor the levels of the streams in their areas and issue local flood forecasts and advisories as necessary. Knowing and understanding the runoff patterns and behaviors of rivers is one of the most challenging jobs in the NWS. It requires a combined knowledge of meteorology, hydrology, and engineering in order to understand seasonal changes and other factors that affect stream behavior.

CLIMATE INFORMATION

The National Climatic Data Center is the official federal repository for all weather observations gathered throughout the United States. The center publishes monthly and annual reports for each of the states. It also disseminates data and information to state and regional climate centers.

The National Climatic Data Center is also the official outlet for other types of historical weather data generated by the U.S. government. For example, copies of past weather maps, weather-satellite pictures, or radar images are available on request from the center. Certain weather data and climate information produced by the military weather services is also available there.

Anyone who wishes to review the past record of Kentucky's weather will find it conveniently summarized in monthly and annual government publications available from the center. These are accessible via the Internet at http://www.ncdc.noaa.gov, where there are a number of options for summarizing and visualizing the data. It is also possible to receive a variety of climate-summary publications on a regular subscription basis. The climate information consists of long-term averages of weather conditions or statistical studies of the probability of certain weather elements occurring. This information is important to engineers, planners, and others whose work is affected by the weather.

In 1978, a memorandum of agreement between the federal government and Western Kentucky University established a cooperative program creating the Office of State Climatology on the university's Bowling Green campus. Western Kentucky University does not have a meteorology department, so responsibility for the state climatology office falls to the Department of Geography and Geology, which appoints the state climatologist. The state climatology office is a source of Kentucky climate data and information, some of which is available at no charge, and some of which (certain more-detailed reports) must be purchased. More information about the Kentucky climate office and its services can be found at http://kyclim.wku.edu.

NOAA has also worked to set up regional climate centers in certain universities where research can be done using weather data and observations. Kentucky is one of eight states in the Midwest served by the Midwestern Regional Climate Center at the University of Illinois. The center publishes research reports describing the climate of that part of the United States. Its Internet site can be found at http://mcc.sws.uiuc.edu, where summarized climatic data for many locations in Kentucky are available.

AGRICULTURAL WEATHER SERVICES

The agricultural sector is one of the most sensitive sectors of the American economy, owing largely to the influence that weather has over it. Farmers must always be alert to the potential damaging effects that weather can have on their crops and livestock. Historically, tobacco was the major cash crop in Kentucky, and, as we have seen, it is sensitive to the vagaries of the weather during nearly every stage of its production. In 1968, the Weather Bureau established a program of specialized weather services for farmers in Kentucky and several other states. The federal program was discontinued in 1976 and subsequently reestablished by the University of Kentucky as the Agricultural Weather Center within the Department of Biosystems and Agricultural Engineering in the College of Agriculture.

Part of the network of cooperative weather observers in Kentucky includes special agricultural-weather-observing stations located in rural areas of the state. Their daily reports feed the College of Agriculture's weather computers, providing data not only on temperature and precipitation but also on elements important to farm production, such as relative humidity, soil temperature, and, in some cases, the amount of evaporation from an open water surface. The information is used by the Agricultural Weather Center to prepare specialized forecasts for current agricultural activities, including pest advisories, crop-spraying advisories, and soil-moisture calculations.

Some of the agricultural-weather-observing stations are located at the experiment station farms operated by the College of Agriculture. These stations provide valuable information about the crop- and livestock-producing environment that aids researchers in understanding how weather affects specific aspects of agricultural production.

ROADWAY WEATHER

The state of Kentucky has joined the federal government as a provider of weather information. The Kentucky Transportation Cabinet has installed a network of weather sensors on the highways of Kentucky and implemented a roadway weather system. The Roadway Weather Information System provides information to the cabinet's maintenance engineers to assist them in deciding what method and what type of chemicals should be used to remove snow and ice. Other users of the system include the NWS, which issues warnings for hazardous driving conditions.

The roadway information system consists of sensors that measure meteorological parameters, including wind direction, wind speed, air temperature, solar radiation, precipitation amount, and

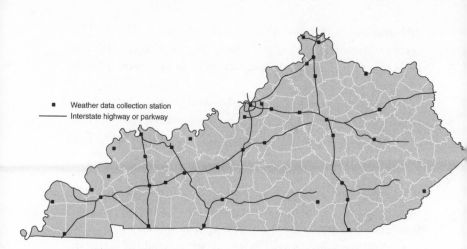

FIGURE 44. *The Kentucky Roadway Weather Information System.*
(Data provided by Kentucky Transportation Cabinet.)

relative humidity. Additionally, there is a simple sensor that can detect dew, sleet, or drizzle on the pavement before it shows up on the precipitation sensor. The information for each location is available on the Internet at http://www.kytc.state.ky.us/RWIS. The map in figure 44 shows the locations where Roadway Weather Information System packages have been installed across the state.

Appendix

TABLE A3. KENTUCKY NORMAL DAILY LOW TEMPERATURES, 1971–2000

NORMAL DAILY LOW TEMPERATURE (°F)

LOCATION	JAN.	FEB.	MAR.	APR.	MAY	JUN.	JUL.	AUG.	SEP.	OCT.	NOV.	DEC.	ANNUAL
Ashland	19.0	20.9	28.8	36.8	46.5	56.2	61.3	59.3	52.3	40.1	30.7	23.2	39.6
Baxter	23.8	26.2	33.1	40.3	50.2	59.3	64.1	62.8	56.2	43.3	33.9	27.2	43.4
Beaver Dam	23.9	27.7	36.0	44.3	53.8	62.8	66.8	64.7	57.3	45.1	36.9	28.3	45.6
Berea	25.6	28.7	36.3	44.5	53.4	61.2	64.6	62.7	56.6	46.1	38.2	29.6	45.6
Bowling Green	25.4	28.6	36.9	45.0	54.5	63.4	67.7	65.7	58.1	45.7	37.2	29.2	46.5
Carrollton	24.0	26.8	35.0	43.5	52.7	61.3	65.9	64.5	58.0	46.1	37.8	28.7	45.4
Covington	21.3	25.0	33.8	42.7	52.9	61.6	66.1	64.2	56.8	44.9	35.7	26.4	44.3
Cynthiana	20.9	23.6	31.5	39.7	49.9	59.4	63.8	61.8	54.2	41.5	33.6	25.5	42.1
Frankfort	20.8	23.0	30.7	39.3	49.3	58.7	63.4	61.9	54.5	42.1	33.9	25.5	41.9
Glasgow	26.3	29.7	37.5	45.1	54.2	62.6	66.7	64.8	58.1	46.3	37.9	30.3	46.6
Greensburg	23.4	25.8	34.0	42.2	52.1	61.7	66.1	63.9	56.3	43.3	35.2	27.3	44.3
Henderson	23.6	27.3	35.8	44.7	54.2	62.8	66.7	64.4	57.2	46.1	37.4	28.0	45.7
Hodgenville	24.7	28.3	36.3	44.0	52.7	60.8	64.9	63.3	56.6	45.2	37.0	28.6	45.2
Hopkinsville	24.4	27.5	37.1	46.4	55.7	64.2	67.9	65.8	58.0	46.3	37.7	28.4	46.6

TABLE A1. *(continued)*

LOCATION	NORMAL DAILY LOW TEMPERATURE (°F)												
	JAN.	FEB.	MAR.	APR.	MAY	JUN.	JUL.	AUG.	SEP.	OCT.	NOV.	DEC.	ANNUAL
Jackson	25.7	28.9	37.4	45.8	54.3	61.9	65.7	64.3	58.4	47.4	38.9	30.2	46.6
Lexington	24.1	27.7	35.9	44.1	53.6	62.2	66.4	64.9	57.9	46.4	37.3	28.4	45.7
London	25.2	28.1	35.7	43.4	52.5	61.0	65.5	63.9	56.9	44.3	36.2	29.1	45.2
Louisville	24.9	28.5	37.1	46.0	56.1	65.1	69.8	68.2	60.9	48.5	39.3	29.9	47.9
Madisonville	25.2	28.8	37.6	46.1	55.3	63.4	67.4	65.5	58.7	46.9	38.3	29.2	46.9
Mayfield	26.3	30.1	38.4	46.4	55.6	64.0	68.1	66.0	58.8	47.0	38.7	30.1	47.5
Maysville	21.3	23.4	31.0	39.7	49.9	59.6	64.5	63.3	56.3	44.2	35.0	26.6	42.9
Monticello	23.6	25.9	33.5	40.6	50.6	60.0	64.3	62.4	55.5	43.1	34.7	27.8	43.5
Mount Sterling	22.0	24.5	32.9	41.1	52.5	61.3	65.6	63.4	56.0	43.7	35.0	26.6	43.7
Murray	26.9	30.9	39.3	48.1	57.2	65.5	69.4	67.4	60.4	48.7	39.4	30.6	48.7
Owensboro	24.4	28.5	36.8	45.4	54.8	63.8	67.7	65.4	58.3	46.2	37.3	28.6	46.4
Paducah	23.9	28.2	37.1	45.6	55.0	63.8	67.7	64.9	57.1	45.2	36.5	27.5	46.0
Princeton	25.6	29.6	38.1	46.7	55.4	64.0	67.9	66.1	59.0	47.4	39.0	30.0	47.4
Russellville	24.6	26.9	35.6	43.6	53.1	61.4	66.3	64.3	57.0	44.6	37.5	28.8	45.3
West Liberty	19.2	21.0	28.9	36.5	46.4	56.1	60.9	59.4	51.3	37.8	30.0	23.5	39.3

Source: Midwestern Regional Climate Center.

TABLE A2. KENTUCKY NORMAL DAILY HIGH TEMPERATURES, 1971–2000

NORMAL DAILY HIGH TEMPERATURE (°F)

LOCATION	JAN.	FEB.	MAR.	APR.	MAY	JUN.	JUL.	AUG.	SEP.	OCT.	NOV.	DEC.	ANNUAL
Ashland	41.6	46.6	57.1	67.9	76.9	84.3	87.9	86.6	80.2	69.3	57.0	46.2	66.8
Baxter	44.0	48.6	58.2	67.9	75.6	82.4	85.9	84.9	78.8	68.5	57.9	48.0	66.7
Beaver Dam	43.3	49.8	59.9	70.0	77.7	85.1	88.5	87.6	81.8	71.5	58.6	47.7	68.5
Berea	43.7	49.4	59.0	68.9	76.5	83.6	87.0	85.9	79.8	68.9	57.3	47.9	67.3
Bowling Green	43.0	48.6	58.6	68.6	77.0	85.3	89.2	87.8	81.8	70.1	57.6	47.4	67.9
Carrollton	41.6	47.7	57.6	67.7	76.3	84.0	87.8	86.6	81.8	70.2	57.6	46.2	67.0
Covington	38.0	43.1	53.9	64.7	74.4	82.4	86.4	84.8	78.0	66.4	53.6	42.7	64.0
Cynthiana	39.7	44.9	55.2	65.6	75.2	83.5	87.4	86.2	80.0	68.4	55.4	44.5	65.5
Frankfort	39.8	44.8	55.3	65.6	74.6	82.6	86.9	85.8	79.4	68.1	55.4	44.4	65.2
Glasgow	45.9	51.9	61.9	71.8	79.8	87.3	90.5	89.4	83.3	72.4	59.7	50.0	70.3
Greensburg	43.5	49.1	58.8	68.8	77.4	85.1	89.2	88.1	82.0	71.1	58.6	48.0	68.3
Henderson	41.5	47.6	58.3	68.7	77.4	85.3	88.4	87.5	81.5	71.1	57.2	45.6	67.5
Hodgenville	43.1	49.5	59.5	69.1	76.5	83.7	87.3	86.4	80.7	70.3	57.8	47.2	67.6
Hopkinsville	41.9	47.8	58.0	68.2	76.5	84.6	88.5	87.6	81.5	70.6	58.0	46.5	67.5

TABLE A2. *(continued)*

NORMAL DAILY HIGH TEMPERATURE (°F)

LOCATION	JAN.	FEB.	MAR.	APR.	MAY	JUN.	JUL.	AUG.	SEP.	OCT.	NOV.	DEC.	ANNUAL
Jackson	42.0	46.8	56.8	66.8	73.8	80.8	84.2	83.3	77.4	67.5	56.4	46.3	65.2
Lexington	39.9	45.2	55.3	65.1	74.0	82.3	85.9	84.6	78.1	66.9	54.5	44.3	64.7
London	43.5	49.3	58.5	67.9	75.5	82.5	86.0	84.8	78.8	68.6	57.5	47.9	66.7
Louisville	41.0	46.6	56.8	66.8	75.4	83.3	87.0	85.8	79.4	68.4	55.9	45.4	66.0
Madisonville	44.3	50.8	61.4	72.0	80.1	87.7	91.2	90.2	84.3	73.2	59.7	48.4	70.3
Mayfield	43.9	50.7	60.9	70.8	78.4	85.9	89.2	88.2	82.2	72.3	58.8	47.9	69.1
Maysville	39.8	44.6	55.0	65.5	75.0	83.2	87.0	85.8	79.7	68.3	55.6	44.8	65.4
Monticello	42.8	48.2	57.6	66.9	74.9	82.6	86.2	85.5	79.8	69.4	57.6	47.5	66.6
Mount Sterling	40.1	46.0	55.7	66.1	75.0	82.4	85.8	84.4	78.5	67.5	55.7	44.9	65.2
Murray	43.8	50.2	60.2	70.3	78.2	86.3	89.9	88.7	82.1	71.4	58.4	47.9	69.0
Owensboro	42.6	49.1	59.5	70.3	79.1	87.4	90.7	89.5	83.4	72.7	58.5	47.1	69.2
Paducah	41.9	48.0	58.1	68.4	76.9	85.2	88.6	87.4	81.2	70.8	57.2	46.3	67.5
Princeton	45.4	51.5	62.0	72.0	80.0	88.0	91.6	90.5	84.4	74.0	60.7	49.7	70.8
Russellville	43.0	47.9	58.5	68.1	76.8	84.9	88.9	87.6	81.3	70.4	58.2	47.3	67.7
West Liberty	42.5	47.9	57.8	68.1	76.3	83.4	87.2	86.0	80.0	69.7	57.9	47.3	67.0

Source: Midwestern Regional Climate Center.

TABLE A3. KENTUCKY TEMPERATURE STATISTICS*

LOCATION	NORMAL ANNUAL TEMPERATURE (°F)	RECORD TEMPERATURE EXTREMES (°F) HIGHEST	DATE	LOWEST	DATE	NORMAL NUMBER OF DAYS ANNUALLY WHEN: HIGH ≥ 90°F	HIGH ≤ 32°F	LOW ≤ 32°F	LOW ≤ 0°F
Ashland	53.2	107	Jul. 28, 1930	−25	Jan. 19, 1994	36	17	134	4
Baxter	55.1	101	Aug. 22, 1983	−19	Jan. 21, 1985	17	11	108	3
Beaver Dam	57.1	110	Sep. 6, 1925	−25	Jan. 24, 1963	38	13	89	2
Berea	56.5	108	Jul. 28, 1930	−21	Jan. 19, 1994	22	13	85	2
Bowling Green	57.2	113	Jul. 28, 1930	−21	Jan. 23, 1963	43	14	89	2
Carrollton	56.2	105	Jul. 27, 1952	−22	Jan. 17, 1977	26	14	98	3
Covington	54.2	103	Jul. 14, 1954	−25	Jan. 18, 1977	18	26	106	5
Cynthiana	53.8	106	Aug. 21, 1983	−33	Jan. 19, 1994	31	18	115	3
Frankfort	53.6	111	Jul. 15, 1936	−27	Jan. 19, 1994	26	18	116	4
Glasgow	58.5	105	Jul. 9, 1988	−25	Jan. 24, 1963	41	14	85	2
Greensburg	56.3	114	Jul. 28, 1930	−29	Feb. 13, 1899	44	13	108	3
Henderson	56.6	113	Jul. 13, 1936	−20	Jan. 19, 1994	36	16	85	2
Hodgenville	56.4	107	Jul. 23, 1983	−25	Jan. 21, 1984	26	13	92	3
Hopkinsville	57.1	111	Aug. 9, 1930	−22	Feb. 2, 1951	43	16	97	2
Jackson	55.9	102	Jul. 17, 1980	−18	Jan. 20, 1985	15	17	81	1
Lexington	55.2	108	Jul. 10, 1936	−21	Jan. 24, 1963	20	21	93	2

TABLE A3. (continued)

LOCATION	NORMAL ANNUAL TEMPERATURE (°F)	RECORD TEMPERATURE EXTREMES (°F)				NORMAL NUMBER OF DAYS ANNUALLY WHEN:			
		HIGHEST	DATE	LOWEST	DATE	HIGH ≥ 90°F	HIGH ≤ 32°F	LOW ≤ 32°F	LOW ≤ 0°F
London	56.0	101	Jul. 9, 1988	−25	Jan. 19, 1994	18	14	93	2
Louisville	56.9	106	Jul. 30, 1999	−22	Jan. 19, 1994	33	18	83	1
Madisonville	58.6	105	Jun. 30, 1952	−23	Feb. 2, 1951	51	13	85	2
Mayfield	58.3	103	Jul. 15, 1980	−18	Jan. 17, 1982	46	10	84	1
Maysville	54.2	108	Jul. 22, 1901	−25	Jan. 19, 1994	27	20	117	3
Monticello	55.1	103	Jul. 10, 1988	−33	Jan. 30, 1963	22	12	96	2
Mount Sterling	54.5	109	Jul. 28, 1930	−22	Feb. 10, 1899	17	16	103	2
Murray	58.8	110	Jul. 27, 1930	−20	Jan. 18, 1930	47	12	76	1
Owensboro	57.8	107	Jun. 28, 1944	−23	Jan. 19, 1994	46	14	87	3
Paducah	56.8	106	Jun. 30, 1952	−15	Jan. 20, 1985	45	15	85	2
Princeton	59.1	105	Jul. 30, 1999	−32	Feb. 2, 1951	48	11	82	2
Russellville	56.6	108	Jul. 28, 1930	−22	Feb. 13, 1899	41	15	102	2
West Liberty	53.2	107	Jun. 20, 1994	−30	Jan. 19, 1994	29	14	135	5

Source: Midwestern Regional Climate Center.

* Normals are based on 1971–2000. Extremes are based on entire length of record.

TABLE A4. KENTUCKY NORMAL PRECIPITATION, 1971–2000

LOCATION	JAN.	FEB.	MAR.	APR.	MAY	JUN.	JUL.	AUG.	SEP.	OCT.	NOV.	DEC.	ANNUAL
Ashland	3.23	3.07	3.78	3.33	4.47	4.02	4.68	3.73	2.83	2.81	3.37	3.60	42.92
Baxter	4.48	4.00	4.88	4.18	5.28	4.51	4.62	4.36	3.22	3.18	4.12	4.35	51.18
Beaver Dam	3.65	4.33	4.65	4.42	5.17	3.72	4.25	3.16	3.69	3.14	4.38	4.47	49.03
Berea	3.23	3.15	4.41	3.84	5.27	4.45	4.08	4.09	3.87	3.10	3.72	4.12	47.33
Bowling Green	4.15	4.15	4.97	3.99	5.36	4.29	4.54	3.36	4.13	3.17	4.46	5.06	51.63
Carrollton	3.26	3.60	4.43	4.40	4.85	3.48	3.61	2.74	3.21	2.67	3.88	4.02	45.20
Covington	2.92	2.75	3.90	3.96	4.59	4.42	3.75	3.79	2.82	2.96	3.46	3.28	42.60
Cynthiana	3.12	3.12	4.25	3.94	4.59	4.18	3.99	3.40	2.92	2.83	3.31	3.83	43.48
Elkhorn City	3.39	3.16	3.80	3.93	4.57	4.28	4.41	4.49	3.42	2.62	3.22	2.92	44.21
Frankfort	3.15	3.08	4.04	3.67	4.61	4.40	4.18	3.58	3.15	2.66	3.33	3.71	43.56
Glasgow	4.29	4.32	5.12	4.37	5.30	4.89	4.78	3.96	3.98	3.17	4.49	5.14	53.81
Greensburg	4.17	4.31	5.07	4.27	5.68	4.87	4.63	3.96	4.03	3.13	4.19	4.95	53.26
Henderson	3.00	3.16	4.45	4.51	4.90	4.05	3.77	2.95	3.34	2.80	4.20	3.64	44.77
Hodgenville	3.73	4.20	4.67	4.34	5.36	4.43	4.48	3.78	4.06	3.33	4.43	4.73	51.54
Hopkinsville	4.08	4.36	5.12	4.38	5.15	3.76	4.05	3.33	3.47	3.28	4.83	5.11	50.92

TABLE A4. *(continued)*

NORMAL PRECIPITATION (INCHES)

LOCATION	JAN.	FEB.	MAR.	APR.	MAY	JUN.	JUL.	AUG.	SEP.	OCT.	NOV.	DEC.	ANNUAL
Jackson	3.56	3.68	4.38	3.79	5.16	4.67	4.59	4.13	3.77	3.18	4.20	4.27	49.38
Lexington	3.34	3.27	4.41	3.67	4.78	4.58	4.81	3.77	3.11	2.70	3.44	4.03	45.91
London	4.01	3.72	4.61	4.01	4.69	4.24	4.39	3.36	3.37	2.80	3.90	4.31	47.41
Louisville	3.28	3.25	4.41	3.91	4.88	3.76	4.30	3.41	3.05	2.79	3.81	3.69	44.54
Madisonville	3.69	3.78	4.51	4.85	4.95	3.80	4.21	3.23	3.36	3.26	4.22	4.21	48.07
Mayfield	3.76	4.48	4.93	4.77	5.05	4.12	4.32	3.23	3.62	3.65	4.96	4.89	51.78
Maysville	3.52	3.24	4.10	3.94	4.87	3.98	4.45	3.79	3.16	2.84	3.38	3.92	45.19
Monticello	4.39	4.08	4.85	4.24	5.15	4.41	4.42	3.82	3.72	2.95	4.15	4.80	50.98
Mount Sterling	3.56	3.39	4.07	3.66	4.80	4.39	5.11	4.00	3.63	2.83	3.38	3.82	46.64
Murray	4.25	4.59	5.25	5.09	5.39	4.85	4.50	3.46	3.64	3.52	5.41	5.34	55.29
Owensboro	3.47	3.85	4.26	4.66	4.78	3.62	3.82	3.54	3.51	3.01	4.10	3.91	46.53
Paducah	3.47	3.93	4.27	4.95	4.75	4.51	4.45	2.99	3.56	3.45	4.53	4.38	49.24
Princeton	4.01	4.48	4.70	4.70	5.01	4.06	4.52	3.56	3.28	3.28	4.80	5.05	51.45
Russellville	4.04	4.09	5.05	3.88	5.65	4.75	3.70	3.14	3.80	3.11	4.44	4.84	50.49
West Liberty	3.48	3.09	4.01	3.61	4.84	4.00	5.07	3.49	3.10	2.82	3.31	4.02	44.84

Source: Midwestern Regional Climate Center.

TABLE A5. KENTUCKY PRECIPITATION STATISTICS*

LOCATION	NORMAL ANNUAL (INCHES)	WETTEST YEAR AMOUNT	WETTEST YEAR YEAR	DRIEST YEAR AMOUNT	DRIEST YEAR YEAR	GREATEST 1 DAY AMOUNT	GREATEST 1 DAY DATE	AVERAGE NUMBER OF DAYS WITH: ≥0.01"	≥0.5"	≥1.0"	SNOWFALL MEAN ANNUAL	SNOWFALL GREATEST 1-DAY	SNOWFALL DATE	AVERAGE NUMBER OF DAYS ≥1 INCH
Ashland	42.92	61.46	1989	23.28	1930	5.61	Jul. 20, 1973	126	29	9	7.8	24.0	Mar. 14, 1993	3
Baxter	51.18	63.26	1989	34.56	1965	5.03	Oct. 2, 1977	127	36	13	10.4	12.0	Feb. 15, 1986	4
Beaver Dam	49.03	76.44	1979	25.20	1903	6.45	Sep. 27, 2002	114	34	13	10.8	12.0	Jan. 17, 1994	3
Berea	47.33	63.53	1979	24.23	1930	5.38	Jun. 12, 1923	130	32	11	11.7	18.5	Feb. 4, 1998	4
Bowling Green	51.63	76.56	1979	25.80	1999	6.15	Dec. 7, 1924	124	33	14	10.4	18.0	Mar. 9, 1960	4
Carrollton	45.20	63.88	1996	23.78	1934	8.30	Apr. 11, 1947	126	31	11	11.3	12.0	Mar. 23, 1968	3
Covington	42.60	57.58	1990	27.99	1963	5.21	Mar. 9, 1964	133	29	9	23.6	11.8	Apr. 2, 1998	7
Cynthiana	43.48	58.21	1975	23.79	1930	4.88	Sep. 1, 1965	115	30	10	8.9	22.0	Jan. 18, 1994	3
Elkhorn City	44.21	58.76	1972	25.98	1955	4.60	Mar. 12, 1963	116	30	11	13.4	13.0	Feb. 19, 1960	5
Frankfort	43.56	60.61	1935	19.87	1901	4.92	Jun. 18, 1927	121	30	11	7.4	17.0	Jan. 18, 1994	2
Glasgow	53.81	67.38	1974	24.47	1953	5.83	Mar. 12, 1975	128	36	15	11.4	16.0	Mar. 9, 1960	4
Greensburg	53.26	68.02	1935	28.96	1901	8.05	Aug. 1, 1967	121	37	15	6.5	12.0	Mar. 9, 1960	3
Henderson	44.77	71.01	1950	28.25	1963	6.33	Mar. 11, 1935	115	31	11	14.4	11.0	Feb. 11, 1985	5
Hodgenville	51.54	67.92	1979	36.83	1999	5.72	Nov. 5, 1948	98	36	14	7.7	15.0	Feb. 11, 1966	3
Hopkinsville	50.92	71.97	1979	28.47	1963	7.06	Mar. 2, 1997	120	35	14	9.7	12.0	Mar. 9, 1960	3
Jackson	49.38	63.29	1989	34.37	2001	3.84	Aug. 24, 1999	144	34	12	24.5	19.8	Mar. 13, 1993	7

TABLE A5. *(continued)*

| LOCATION | NORMAL ANNUAL (INCHES) | WETTEST YEAR | | DRIEST YEAR | | GREATEST 1 DAY | | AVERAGE NUMBER OF DAYS WITH: | | | SNOWFALL | | | |
		AMOUNT	YEAR	AMOUNT	YEAR	AMOUNT	DATE	≥ 0.01"	≥ 0.5"	≥ 1.0"	MEAN ANNUAL	GREATEST 1-DAY	DATE	AVERAGE NUMBER OF DAYS ≥ 1 INCH
Lexington	45.91	66.46	1935	24.89	1930	8.04	Aug. 2, 1932	131	31	11	15.7	10.0	Jan. 17, 1994	4
London	47.41	62.02	1979	27.11	1999	4.78	Oct. 1, 1977	136	33	11	14.0	15.0	Mar. 9, 1960	6
Louisville	44.54	59.80	1979	30.38	1953	7.22	Mar. 1, 1997	126	30	11	14.6	15.5	Jan. 17, 1994	4
Madisonville	48.07	63.23	1950	26.29	1963	10.25	Mar. 2, 1997	116	32	13	6.5	13.5	Jan. 17, 1994	2
Mayfield	51.78	71.80	1979	27.49	2001	5.70	Mar. 1, 1997	110	36	15	8.2	10.0	Mar. 22, 1968	2
Maysville	45.19	59.52	1935	19.26	1901	6.28	Jul. 14, 1938	130	31	10	4.5	16.0	Jan. 17, 1994	1
Monticello	50.98	68.16	1989	31.16	1985	4.80	Jun. 20, 1946	130	35	13	16.2	11.0	Mar. 9, 1960	5
Mount Sterling	46.64	70.32	1909	22.43	1930	6.00	Dec. 8, 1978	116	32	12	8.4	9.3	Feb. 10, 1964	3
Murray	55.29	72.39	1990	27.79	1941	6.81	Mar. 1, 1997	111	37	16	10.8	10.6	Mar. 22, 1968	3
Owensboro	46.53	61.40	1923	23.61	1997	5.40	Mar. 19, 1943	107	33	12	8.5	15.0	Dec. 23, 2004	3
Paducah	49.24	70.58	1950	28.2	1963	7.49	Sep. 5, 1985	110	33	14	10.2	14.0	Dec. 23, 2004	4
Princeton	51.45	71.61	1979	34.11	1986	5.48	Feb. 15, 1990	121	34	14	13.5	14.0	Jan. 17, 1994	5
Russellville	50.49	75.21	1950	22.04	1918	8.80	Jun. 23, 1969	108	39	15	9.0	15.2	Mar. 9, 1960	3
West Liberty	44.84	72.54	1950	28.44	1963	5.90	Sep. 20, 1950	114	31	10	6.0	16.0	Feb. 13, 1985	2

Source: Midwestern Regional Climate Center.

* Normals are based on 1971–2000. Extremes are based on entire length of record.

TABLE A6. AVERAGE NUMBER OF DAYS WITH 0.01 INCHES OR MORE OF PRECIPITATION, 1971–2000

LOCATION	JAN.	FEB.	MAR.	APR.	MAY	JUN.	JUL.	AUG.	SEP.	OCT.	NOV.	DEC.	TOTAL
Ashland	11	10	12	12	12	11	10	9	8	8	11	12	126
Baxter	12	11	12	11	12	11	11	10	9	8	10	12	127
Bowling Green	12	11	13	11	12	10	9	8	9	8	10	12	124
Covington	13	12	13	13	12	12	10	10	8	9	11	12	133
Henderson	10	9	12	12	11	10	8	7	8	8	10	11	115
Hopkinsville	11	10	12	11	12	10	9	8	8	8	11	11	120
Lexington	12	11	13	12	12	11	11	9	9	8	11	12	131
Louisville	11	11	13	12	12	10	10	8	9	8	11	12	126
Mayfield	10	9	11	11	11	9	8	7	8	7	10	10	110
Paducah	9	9	11	11	11	9	8	7	7	8	10	10	110

Source: Midwestern Regional Climate Center.

TABLE A7. KENTUCKY EXTREME RAINFALL AMOUNTS (INCHES)

LOCATION	6-HOUR DURATION			12-HOUR DURATION			24-HOUR DURATION		
	1 IN 10 YEARS	1 IN 50 YEARS	1 IN 100 YEARS	1 IN 10 YEARS	1 IN 50 YEARS	1 IN 100 YEARS	1 IN 10 YEARS	1 IN 50 YEARS	1 IN 100 YEARS
Ashland	3	4	4.5	3.5	4.5	5	4	5	6
Bowling Green	4	5.5	6	4.75	6	7	5.5	7	8
Covington	3.25	4.5	5	3.75	5	6	4.25	6	7
Henderson	3.75	5.5	6	4.25	6	7	5	7	8
Hopkinsville	4	5.5	6	4.75	6	7	5.5	7	8
Lexington	3.25	4.5	5	4	5	5.5	4.5	6	6.5
London	3.5	5	6	4	5.5	6.5	4.5	6.5	7.5
Louisville	3.5	5	5.25	4.25	5.5	6.5	4.75	6.5	7
Paducah	4	5.5	6	4.75	6	7	5.5	7.5	8
Pikeville	3	4	4.5	3.5	4.5	5	4	5	6

Source: Midwestern Climate Center, Research Report 92-03, Rainfall Frequency Atlas of the Midwest, 1992.

TABLE A8. RECORD DAILY LOW TEMPERATURES RECORDED IN KENTUCKY

DATE	LOCATION	LOW TEMPERATURE (°F)
January 19, 1994	Shelbyville	−37
February 2, 1951	Princeton	−32
March 6, 1960	Bonnieville	−14
April 2, 1857	Millersburg	10
May 10, 1966	Falmouth	20
June 1, 1966	Cumberland	29
July 1, 1988	Ashland	34
August 31, 1946	Clermont	36
September 26, 1928	Farmers	24
October 27, 1962	Dewey Dam	10
November 30, 1929	Shelbyville	−9
December 24, 1989	Farmers	−24

Source: Kentucky Climate Center.

TABLE A9. RECORD DAILY HIGH TEMPERATURES RECORDED IN KENTUCKY

DATE	LOCATION	HIGH TEMPERATURE (°F)
January 20, 1907	Loretto	83
February 11, 1890	Princeton	86
March 24, 1929	Hopkinsville	94
April 24, 1925	Farmers	98
May 10, 1896	Ashland	106
June 29, 1936	Saint John's Academy (Hardin County)	110
July 28, 1930	Greensburg	114
August 5, 1930	Saint John's Academy (Hardin County)	113
September 6, 1925	Beaver Dam	110
October 1, 1953	Frankfort and Hopkinsville	98
November 14, 1902	Pikeville	90
December 3, 1982	Pikeville	87

Source: Kentucky Climate Center.

TABLE A10. KENTUCKY FREEZE DATA, 1971–2000*

LOCATION	SPRING DATE			FALL DATE			LENGTH OF SEASON (DAYS)		
	AVERAGE	EARLIEST	LATEST	AVERAGE	EARLIEST	LATEST	AVERAGE	SHORTEST	LONGEST
Ashland	May 4	Apr. 11	Jun. 12	Oct. 12	Sep. 23	Nov. 12	164	138	243
Baxter	Apr. 20	Apr. 1	May 13	Oct. 23	Oct. 3	Nov. 13	185	157	215
Bowling Green	Apr. 10	Mar. 24	May 5	Oct. 21	Oct. 3	Nov. 13	202	167	219
Covington	Apr. 21	Mar. 29	May 16	Oct. 19	Sep. 30	Nov. 8	184	149	212
Henderson	Apr. 10	Mar. 23	Apr. 23	Oct. 22	Oct. 3	Nov. 23	198	175	229
Hopkinsville	Apr. 11	Mar. 23	May 5	Oct. 18	Sep. 21	Nov. 13	192	149	214
Lexington	Apr. 13	Mar. 27	May 5	Oct. 25	Oct. 2	Nov. 13	194	160	216
Louisville	Apr. 8	Mar. 22	May 5	Nov. 3	Oct. 3	Nov. 25	206	167	248
Paducah	Apr. 9	Mar. 7	Apr. 29	Oct. 23	Oct. 3	Nov. 13	200	174	250

Source: Kentucky Agricultural Weather Center.

* Threshold 32°F

TABLE A11. MAXIMUM RAINFALL FOR SELECTED TIME INTERVALS

DURATION	RAINFALL	LOCATION	DATE
5 minutes	0.79 inch	Louisville	August 29, 1917
10 minutes	1.20 inches	Lexington	August 11, 1957
15 minutes	1.54 inches	Lexington	July 3, 1931
30 minutes	2.66 inches	Louisville	July 18, 1971
1 hour	3.87 inches	Berea	June 26, 1943
2 hours	4.70 inches	Middlesboro	July 24, 1965
3 hours	6.3 inches	Fordsville	July 26, 2001
6 hours	8.85 inches	Scottsville	June 23, 1969
12 hours	9.68 inches	Scottsville	June 23, 1969
24 hours	10.48 inches	Louisville	February 28–March 1, 1997

TABLE A12. RECORD GREATEST MONTHLY PRECIPITATION IN KENTUCKY

MONTH	AMOUNT	LOCATION	YEAR
January	22.97 inches	Earlington	1937
February	13.33 inches	Burnside	1890
March	17.82 inches	Sebree	1964
April	16.87 inches	Addison Dam	1970
May	17.10 inches	Elkton	1983
June	19.22 inches	Paducah	1966
July	16.61 inches	Hickman	1972
August	15.50 inches	Alpha	1901
September	15.31 inches	Aberdeen	1979
October	12.92 inches	Warsaw Markland Dam	1983
November	15.62 inches	Cadiz	1957
December	17.64 inches	Jamestown	1978

Source: Kentucky Climate Center.

TABLE A13. KENTUCKY RECORD GREATEST MONTHLY SNOWFALL

MONTH	AMOUNT	LOCATION	YEAR
January	46.0 inches	La Grange	1978
February	30.0 inches	Benham	1960
March	46.5 inches	Benham	1960
April	29.0 inches	Freeburn	1987
May	5.0 inches	Springfield	1894
June	0 inch		
July	0 inch		
August	0 inch		
September	0 inch		
October	7.5 inches	Sergent	1923
November	21.5 inches	Benham	1950
December	28.3 inches	Cherokee Park	1917

Source: Kentucky Climate Center.

TABLE A14. TORNADOES OBSERVED IN KENTUCKY, 1950–2003

INTENSITY	JAN.	FEB.	MAR.	APR.	MAY	JUN.	JUL.	AUG.	SEP.	OCT.	NOV.	DEC.	ANNUAL
						NUMBER OF TORNADOES							
F0 Light damage		3	17	10	35	26	11	8	1		7	1	119
F1 Moderate damage	11	6	15	57	52	33	29	3	7	3	18	2	236
F2 Considerable damage	2	1	24	41	43	18	7	6	2	3	5	6	158
F3 Severe damage	4	1	10	39	16	9					1	2	82
F4 Devastating damage			2	32	1						2		37
F5 Incredible damage				3									3
Total	17	11	68	182	147	86	47	17	10	6	33	11	635

Source: Based on data from the National Climatic Data Center.

TABLE A15. MONTHLY MEAN WIND SPEED (MPH) AND PREVAILING DIRECTION

MONTH	PADUCAH (1949–95) PREVAILING DIRECTION	SPEED	MAXIMUM GUSTS	LOUISVILLE (1948–95) PREVAILING DIRECTION	SPEED	MAXIMUM GUSTS	COVINGTON (1948–95) PREVAILING DIRECTION	SPEED	MAXIMUM GUSTS	LEXINGTON (1948–95) PREVAILING DIRECTION	SPEED	MAXIMUM GUSTS	JACKSON (1981–95) PREVAILING DIRECTION	SPEED	MAXIMUM GUSTS	HUNTINGTON (1961–95) PREVAILING DIRECTION	SPEED	MAXIMUM GUSTS
Jan.	SSW	13	51	S	10	60	SSW	12	71	S	12	78	SW	9	55	W	10	60
Feb.	SSW	12	54	WNW	12	60	SSW	12	55	S	10	56	S	9	60	WSW	9	53
Mar.	SSW	14	60	WNW	13	60	SSW	13	64	S	12	53	S	9	53	WSW	10	54
Apr.	SSW	13	64	S	10	84	SSW	12	71	S	12	61	S	8	58	WSW	10	56
May.	SSW	10	84	S	8	60	SSW	9	59	S	9	59	S	7	49	SW	7	55
Jun.	SSW	9	58	S	7	72	SSW	9	67	S	8	64	SSW	6	60	SW	7	56
Jul.	SSW	9	59	S	7	84	SSW	8	83	S	7	63	S	6	55	SW	7	56
Aug.	SSW	8	51	S	6	59	SSW	7	62	S	7	51	S	6	49	SW	7	49
Sep.	SSW	9	52	S	7	55	SSW	8	54	S	8	52	S	6	39	SW	7	46
Oct.	SSW	10	49	S	8	44	SSW	9	59	S	8	52	S	7	48	ESE	5	39
Nov.	SSW	12	63	S	9	58	SSW	12	56	S	10	56	S	8	52	SW	8	55
Dec.	SSW	12	58	S	9	56	SSW	12	61	S	12	58	SW	8	60	SW	8	62
Annual	SSW	10	84	S	9	84	SSW	10	83	S	9	78	S	7	60	SW	8	62

Source: International Station Meteorological Climate Summary, Federal Climate Complex, U.S. Dept. of Commerce/Department of the Navy/Department of the Air Force, Asheville, N.C.

TABLE A16. THUNDERSTORM FREQUENCY BY MONTH

LOCATION	PERIOD OF RECORD (YEARS)	MEAN NUMBER OF DAYS WITH THUNDERSTORMS												
		JAN.	FEB.	MAR.	APR.	MAY	JUN.	JUL.	AUG.	SEP.	OCT.	NOV.	DEC.	ANNUAL*
Paducah	21	1	2	4	6	9	9	8	7	4	3	2	1	55
Louisville	56	1	1	3	5	7	8	8	7	3	2	2	1	47
Covington	57	1	1	3	4	6	7	8	7	3	1	1	1	43
Lexington	59	1	1	3	4	6	8	8	6	3	1	1	0	43
Jackson	24	1	1	3	5	9	10	11	8	3	1	1	0	52
Huntington, W.V.	41	0	1	3	4	6	7	8	6	2	1	1	0	40
Nashville, Tenn.	61	1	2	4	5	7	8	9	7	4	2	2	1	52

Source: Based on data from the National Climatic Data Center.

* Annual totals may not add owing to rounding.

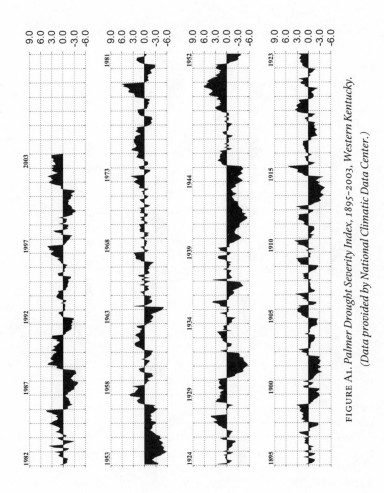

FIGURE A1. *Palmer Drought Severity Index, 1895–2003, Western Kentucky.*
(Data provided by National Climatic Data Center.)

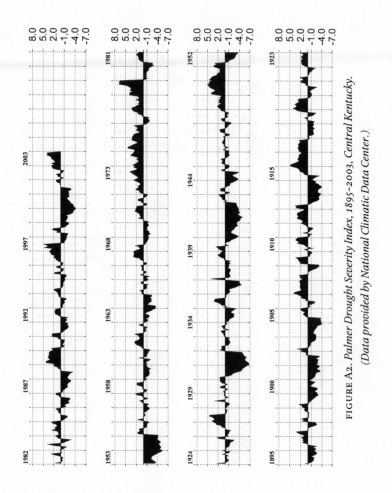

FIGURE A2. *Palmer Drought Severity Index, 1895–2003, Central Kentucky.*
(Data provided by National Climatic Data Center.)

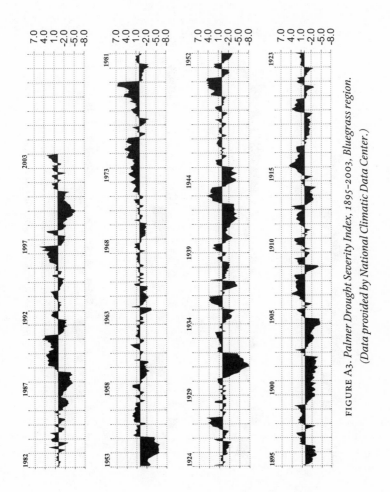

FIGURE A3. *Palmer Drought Severity Index, 1895–2003, Bluegrass region.*
(Data provided by National Climatic Data Center.)

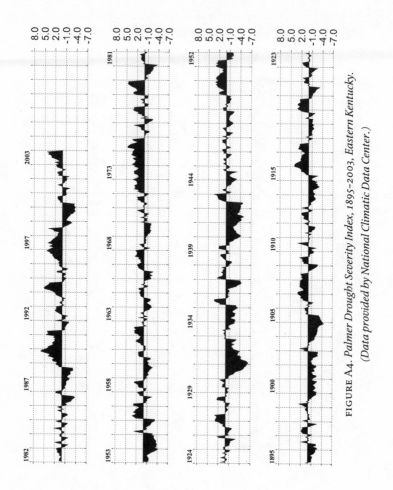

FIGURE A4. *Palmer Drought Severity Index, 1895–2003, Eastern Kentucky. (Data provided by National Climatic Data Center.)*

Bibliographic Essay

Some of the early descriptions of Kentucky's weather that infer a temperate climate can be found in Arthur B. Moore's *The Frontier Mind* (1959) and in Gilbert Imlay's *A Topographical Description of the Western Territory of North America* (1792). Thomas Jefferson also believed that the part of Virginia that lay in present Kentucky had a mild climate, and he described it in his *Notes on the State of Virginia* (1788). The Frenchman Constantin François de Chasseboeuf, comte de Volney, recorded his discussions with Jefferson and similar views about the climate in his *View of the Climate and Soil of the United States of America* (1804).

John Filson provided the first hint that Kentucky has a real winter by writing a chapter on air and climate in his *The Discovery, Settlement, and Present State of Kentucky* (1784). The early concepts of a mild Ohio Valley climate were also challenged by Dr. Daniel Drake, a pioneer physician, who wrote about his assessment in *Notices concerning Cincinnati* (1810).

A description of early weather observations in America can be found in James R. Fleming's *Meteorology in America* (1990).

Lorin Blodget—who in 1851 had become assistant in charge of researches on climatology at the Smithsonian Institution—attempted the first realistic description of the region's climate. In 1857, he published *The Climatology of the United States and of the Temperate Latitudes of the North American Continent*. The *North American Review* of January 1858 said about the book: "As a contribution to science, its importance cannot be overrated." It was extensively circulated, and five hundred copies that were sent to Europe were sold in just 6 months.

The first actual government records of the weather in Kentucky were kept at the Newport Army Barracks in Newport, Kentucky. The records were microfilmed by the National Archives: batch no. AE 04490, CL-689, Newport (50 pages), and Newport Barracks,

Kentucky (249 pages). The Kentucky Climate Center at Western Kentucky University has copies of the microfilm. The instructions of Joseph Lovell, the army surgeon general in 1818, that each army surgeon keep a diary of the weather are in Charles Smart's *The Connection of the Army Medical Department with the Development of Meteorology in the United States* (1894).

Early narrative descriptions of Kentucky weather can be found in a number of newspapers and writings from the nineteenth century. The account by B. O. Gaines of the weather in 1816 can be found in his *History of Scott County* (1905). Comments from Jesse Graddy about the severe winter of 1789 were found in an 1842 interview. See Lucien Beckner's "John D. Shane's Interview with Jesse Graddy of Woodford County" (1946). Richard Collins's *History of Kentucky* (1874) provided valuable insight into Kentucky weather by publishing actual weather records of the observer John Younglove. Collins's book also includes narrative descriptions of harsh winter weather conditions encountered by settlers coming to Kentucky via the Ohio River. The narrative description of the siege of Fort Boonesboro that was thwarted by heavy rain can be found on pp. 212-13 of *The Long Hunter* (1976) by Lawrence Elliott.

The account of the severe storms encountered in 1750 has been taken from Dr. Thomas Walker's diary. See Francis Marion Rust, arranger, *Dr. Thomas Walker's Diary of Exploration* (1950), pp. 30-31. The similar account of tornado-like damage seen along the Ohio River in 1779 appeared in John D. Barnhart's *Henry Hamilton and George Rogers Clark in the American Revolution with the Unpublished Journal of Lieut. Gov. Henry Hamilton* (1951).

The extracts from Colonel William Fleming's notes, taken while he was at Fort Boonesboro during the winter of 1779-80, are available in Newton Mereness, ed., *Travels in the American Colonies* (1916). For a more complete description of winters that affected early Americans, readers may wish to consult the two-volume set by David Ludlum *Early American Winters, 1604-1820* (1966) and *Early American Winters, 1821-1870* (1968).

Descriptions of the spas that flourished in Kentucky during the nineteenth century were obtained mainly from J. Winston Coleman's *The Springs of Kentucky* (1955). The description of the last hours of the life of Cassius M. Clay was taken from a speech delivered to the Chicago Civil War Roundtable by the Lexington historian William H. Townsend on October 17, 1952.

Many sources are available to anyone interested in weather sayings and superstitions. The most comprehensive regional collection that I have found is a full chapter about weather sayings in *Kentucky Superstitions* (1920) by Daniel L. Thomas and Lucy B. Thomas. Another interesting early collection can be found in *Rain Making and Other Weather Vagaries* (1926) by William J. Humphreys.

The growth and development of government involvement in weather services is described in Donald Whitnah's *A History of the U.S. Weather Bureau* (1961). I also relied on personal knowledge and individual station summaries that document the sequence of observing locations and instrumentation arrays that have existed in Kentucky. An interesting account of early American meteorology and government weather services can be found in *Braving the Elements* by David Laskin (1996).

A series of U.S. government agency publications describing Kentucky weather and climate in detail and supplying actual summarized data have appeared over the years. Appearing first—both in 1933—were two sections of the U.S. Weather Bureau's *Climatic Summary of the United States: Western Kentucky* (sec. 74) and *Eastern Kentucky* (sec. 75).

In 1941, when the U.S. Weather Bureau was part of the Department of Agriculture, the department issued its annual *Yearbook of Agriculture* under the title *Climate and Man*. Separate chapters were dedicated to each state, with maps and charts of temperature and precipitation. For agricultural interests, there were also tables showing the average dates of the first and last frosts. The chapter titled "Climate of Kentucky" was written by James Kendall, who had also written the 1933 climate summaries.

Climate and Man was followed by a new series of publications in 1959 by the U.S. Weather Bureau called *Climates of the States*. These were separate booklets about each state, including a fifteen-page publication about Kentucky. This time the publication was written by O. K. Anderson, the head of the Louisville office with the dual title of meteorologist in charge and state climatologist for Kentucky.

My *Climate of Kentucky* (1976) appeared as part of the University of Kentucky College of Agriculture's Progress Report series. Over the years, a number of Kentucky-specific studies and publications have been prepared by the various state climatologists about such topics as frost risk, precipitation probabilities, and drought frequency. The Kentucky Climate Center at Western Kentucky University and the Agricultural Weather Center at the University of Kentucky are good sources for this type of information.

Charts and maps of climate elements were initially published by the U.S. Environmental Science Services Administration in a comprehensive folio called *Climatic Atlas of the United States* (1968). While this printed publication is no longer available, similar and more recent charts are available on a CD-ROM from the National Climatic Data Center, also called *Climatic Atlas of the United States* (2002).

The Internet is a valuable source of regional climate information, and there are four main sources of data. The Kentucky Climate Center maintains data for Kentucky only, and its webpage can be found at http://kyclim.wku.edu. The Midwest Climate Center at the University of Illinois maintains a webpage that has data and information for locations in Kentucky and eight other Midwestern states. It can be found at http://mcc.sws.uiuc.edu. The Southeast Regional Climate Center at the South Carolina Department of Natural Resources also provides weather summaries and climate information for Kentucky and ten other states in the Southeast. Its webpage can be found at http://www.dnr.state. sc.us/climate/sercc.

The National Climatic Data Center, operated by the National Oceanic and Atmospheric Administration, is the world's largest archive for weather data and climate information. Some of the summarized data must be purchased, but a large amount can be found at no charge at http://www.ncdc.noaa.gov/oa/ncdc.html.

Bibliography

Barnhart, John D. *Henry Hamilton and George Rogers Clark in the American Revolution with the Unpublished Journal of Lieut. Gov. Henry Hamilton.* Crawfordsville, Ind., 1951.

Beckner, Lucien, ed. "John D. Shane's Interview with Jesse Graddy of Woodford County." *Filson Club History Quarterly* 20, no. 1 (January 1946): 10–17.

Blodget, Lorin. *Climatology of the United States and of the Temperate Latitudes of the North American Continent.* Philadelphia, 1857.

Coleman, J. Winston. *The Springs of Kentucky.* Lexington, Ky., 1955.

Collins, Richard H. *History of Kentucky.* Covington, Ky., 1874.

Drake, Daniel. *Notices concerning Cincinnati.* Cincinnati, 1810.

Elliott, Lawrence. *The Long Hunter.* New York, 1976.

Filson, John. *The Discovery, Settlement, and Present State of Kentucky.* Wilmington, Del., 1784.

Fleming, James R. *Meteorology in America.* Baltimore, 1990.

Gaines, B. O. *History of Scott County.* Georgetown, Ky., 1905.

Hill, J. D. *Climate of Kentucky.* University of Kentucky College of Agriculture Progress Report no. 221. Lexington, Ky., 1976.

Humphreys, William J. *Rain Making and Other Weather Vagaries.* Baltimore, 1926.

Imlay, Gilbert. *A Topographical Description of the Western Territory of North America.* London, 1792.

Jefferson, Thomas. *Notes on the State of Virginia.* Philadelphia, 1788.

Laskin, David. *Braving the Elements.* New York, 1996.

Ludlum, David M. *Early American Winters, 1604–1820.* Boston, 1966.

——. *Early American Winters, 1821–1870.* Boston, 1968.

——. *Weather Record Book.* Princeton, N.J., 1971.

Mereness, Newton, ed. *Travels in the American Colonies.* New York, 1916.

Moore, Arthur B. *The Frontier Mind.* Lexington, Ky., 1959.

National Academy of Sciences. *Understanding Climate Change.* Washington, D.C., 1975.

National Climatic Data Center. *Climatic Atlas of the United States.* Asheville, N.C., 2002. CD-ROM.

Rust, Francis Marion, arranger. *Dr. Thomas Walker's Diary of Exploration.* 5th ed. Barbourville, Ky., 1950.

Smart, Charles. *The Connection of the Army Medical Department with the Development of Meteorology in the United States.* Weather Bureau Bulletin 11. Washington, D.C., 1894.

Thomas, Daniel L., and Lucy B. Thomas. *Kentucky Superstitions.* Princeton, N.J., 1920.

U.S. Department of Agriculture. *Climate and Man.* Washington, D.C., 1941.

U.S. Environmental Science Services Administration. *Climatic Atlas of the United States.* Asheville, N.C., 1968.

U.S. Weather Bureau. *Climatic Summary of the United States.* Sec. 75, *Eastern Kentucky.* Washington, D.C., 1933.

———. *Climatic Summary of the United States.* Sec. 74, *Western Kentucky.* Washington, D.C., 1933.

———. *Substation History—Kentucky.* Washington, D.C., 1956.

———. *Climates of the States—Kentucky.* Washington, D.C., 1959.

Visher, Stephen S. "The Climate of Kentucky." In *The Pleistocene of Northern Kentucky: A Regional Reconnaissance Study of the Physical Effects of Glaciation within the Commonwealth.* Kentucky Geological Survey, Bulletin 31, Ser. 6. Frankfort, Ky., 1929.

Volney, Constantin François de Chasseboeuf, comte de. *View of the Climate and Soil of the United States of America.* London, 1804.

Whitnah, Donald R. *A History of the U.S. Weather Bureau.* Urbana, Ill., 1961.

Index

Brown, Sergeant Thomas J., 143
Burlington (Vt.), 44
Bowdoin College, 32

Caldwell County, 90
Cambridge (Mass.), 31
Campbellsville, 119
Canada, 41
Candlemas Day, 136
canebrakes, 18
Caneyville, 56
carbon dioxide trends, 131
Carlisle County, 97
Carrollton, 15, 76, 106
catastrophic natural disaster,
    defined, 82
Catlettsburg, 73
Charleston (S.C.), 31
China, 12
Christmas icestorm of 1890, 65
Cincinnati, 25, 105, 123, 124, 144
Cincinnati Daily Commercial, 124
Civil Aviation Agency, 149
Clark, George Rogers, 96
Clay, Cassius M., 127
climate, 13, 16
Climate and Man (1941; U.S.
    Department of Agriculture), 37
climate change, 134
climate information, 153
Climate of Kentucky (Hill), 37
Climate of Kentucky (1976;
    University of Kentucky
    Agricultural Experiment
    Station), 38

climate of North America, 15
climatic optimum, 19
Climatic Summary of the United
    States (1933; U.S. Weather
    Bureau), 37
climatologists, 12
climax vegetation, 18
Closplint, 62
clouds, 5
cloud cover, 113
cloud observations, 114
coal, 14
coalfields, 13, 14
cold, 41
cold air masses, 2
cold fronts, 5
cold waves, 41, 42, 43
Colden, Cadwallader, 31
Collins, Richard H. (author,
    History of Kentucky), 36, 123
Columbia Gas Company, 45
continental climate, 40
continental glaciers, 15
cooperative weather observations,
    151
coral, 14, 15
Corydon, 89
cotton production, 119
Covington, 15, 44, 49, 80, 105
Cumberland Gap, 95
Cumberland Plateau, 18
Cumberland River, 71
cumulonimbus clouds, 8
cumulus clouds, 5, 6
Cynthiana, 42, 43

Franklin, 48

Franklin County, 89

Franklin, Benjamin, 31, 139

Freeburn, 63

freeze-free season, 119

freeze-thaw cycles, 52

French explorers, 19

frost and freeze, 11, 50, 119

frost pockets, 10, 11

Frozen Creek flood, 71

Fujita tornado intensity scale, 97, 98

Fujita, Dr. T. Theodore, 97

Fulton County, 16

funnel cloud, 92

Gaines, B. O. (author, *History of Scott County*), 47

Galilei, Galileo, 31

Garden of Eden, 21

geologic clues, 14

glacial periods, 15

glaciation, 15

glaciers, 13, 15, 16

Glasgow, 87

Golden Pond, 42

governor's mansion, 43

Graddy, Jesse, 51

Grant County, 63

grasslands, 19

Gray Hawk, 42

Grayson, 42

Grayson County, 56

great ice age, 15

great lakes, 5

Green River, 58

greenhouse effect, 130

greenhouse gases, 130

Greenland ice cap, 19

Greensburg, 42, 48

Groundhog Day, 136

growing season, defined, 50

growing season, length of, 50

Gulf of Mexico, 5

hail, 84

    damage, 86, 90

    losses, 86

    risk, 86

    size, 86, 87

hailstones, 85

hailstorm of April 16, 1998, 87

Hamilton, Lord Henry, 96

Hardinsburg, 99

Harlan, 71, 90

Harlan County, 8, 97

Hart County, 42

Harvard University, 32

hazardous driving, 6

heat, 48

    heat wave of 1930, 48

    heat wave of 1936, 49

    heat wave of 1999, 49

heat index, 117

Heidelberg, 42

Henderson, 74

Henderson County, 89

Henry County, 89

Henry, Professor Joseph, 36

Hickman, 44

Hickman Creek, 71
high-pressure center, 2
Hillenmeyer family, 36
History of Kentucky (Collins), 36–37
Hopkins County, 56, 58
Hopkinsville, 42, 49
Hunt, William Gibbs, 33
hurricanes, 4, 58
  Hurricane Betsy, 58
  Hurricane Bob, 59
  Hurricane Camille, 58
  Hurricane David, 59
  Hurricane Frances, 59
  Hurricane Frederic, 59
  Hurricane Ivan, 60

ice, 65
ice sheet, 15
icestorms, 6
  icestorm of 1951, 66
  icestorm of 1971, 69
  icestorm of 2003, 69
Illinois glacial stage, 15, 16
Imlay, Gilbert (author, *A
    Topographical Description of
    the Western Territory of North
    America*), 22
Indiana University, 37
insurance losses, 86
interglacial period, 130
Iroquois Indians, 21

Jackson, 62, 145
James River, 58
Japan, 12

Jefferson, Thomas, 23, 31, 32
  author of *Notes on the State of
    Virginia*, 24
Jessamine County, 36
Jillson, W. R., 37

Kendall, J. L., 37
Kentucky Agricultural Weather
    Center, 155
Kentucky Climate Center, 52
Kentucky climate divisions, 38
Kentucky Derby, 126
Kentucky Gazette, 32, 46, 106, 123
Kentucky Geological Survey, 37
Kentucky Horticulture Society, 36
Kentucky Post, 105
Kentucky River, 15, 58, 78, 122
Kentucky spas, 122
Knott County, 97
Knox County, 97
Köppen, Wladimir, 12

La Niña, 134
La Grange, 63
Lake Malone, 57
Lalemant, Hierosme, 21
last freeze, 50
Lawrence County, 97
Lebanon, 43, 90
Letcher County, 63
Lexington, 33, 36, 42, 48, 49, 51, 61,
    62, 64, 65, 69, 71, 72, 84, 108,
    123, 143, 145
Lexington Herald-Leader, 78
Licking River, 15

normal mean annual temperature, 9

normal temperature and precipitation, defined, 38

North American Review, 32

North Korea, 12

Office of State Climatology, 154

official weather observing stations, 29, 31

Ohio River, 13, 15, 44
  floods, 74
  freezing of, 123, 124

Ohio River Valley, 15, 16

Oldham County, 63

Owen County, 89

Owensboro, 19, 50, 84

Pacific Ocean, 5

Paducah, 50, 58, 74, 77, 145

Paintsville, 95

Palmer Drought Severity Index (PDSI), 103, 104

Palmer, W. C., 103

Paris (Ky.), 36

Perry County, 62

Philadelphia, 32

Pike County, 62, 63, 71

Pikeville, 71

Pine Mountain, 6, 61

Pittsburgh, 32, 123

precipitation, 53
  distribution, 53, 56, 60, 81
  diurnal variation, 57
  driest month, 53
  driest year, 56
  greatest monthly, 56
  least normal annual, 56
  return periods, 72, 168*t*
  wettest year, 56

prehistoric sea life, evidence of, 14

pressure, 1
  highest observed, 3
  lowest observed, 3
  rising and falling, 3
  systems, 1, 3, 53

Princeton, 90

Pulaski County, 102

Rafinesque, Professor Constantine, 33

rain, 5, 6. *See also* precipitation

Red Boiling Springs (Tenn.), 57

relative humidity, 115
  defined, 116

resort hotels, 122

Richmond, 42, 44, 65, 71

river and flood forecasts, 152

Roadway Weather Information System, 155

Rockcastle County, 102

Rowan County, 71

Saint Bartholomew's Day, 137

Saint Medard's Day, 137

Saint Protasius's Day, 137

Saint Swithin's Day, 137

Salt Lick Creek, 57

Salyersville, 95

Scottsville, 57